HARVARD STUDIES IN ENGLISH
VOLUME X

CHRISTOPHER MARLOWE IN LONDON

BY

MARK ECCLES

CHRISTOPHER MARLOWE
IN LONDON

BY

MARK ECCLES

1967

OCTAGON BOOKS, INC.

New York

Reprinted 1967

by special arrangement with Harvard University Press

OCTAGON BOOKS, INC.
175 FIFTH AVENUE
NEW YORK, N. Y. 10010

LIBRARY OF CONGRESS CATALOG CARD NUMBER: 67-18761

Printed in U.S.A. by
NOBLE OFFSET PRINTERS, INC.
NEW YORK 3, N. Y.

INTRODUCTION

TO EVERYONE who is involved, even but casually, with the Elizabethans, Dr. Eccles is already well known. His pioneer work on Spenser, Middleton, Buc, and Barnes has proved his extraordinary prowess in the exacting adventure of exploration. All Dr. Eccles's readers will hail the prizes he has captured from oblivion; but there are relatively few who have threaded the stony paths, rough quarries, and rocks of the records sufficiently far to enable them to understand his portance in his travel's history. Discovery is lonely work. Its pains are not to be communicated, its intimate delights cannot be shared.

In this kind of odyssey, *rimari*, *explorare*, and *vestigare* are not enough; to root up, grub through, pry into, seek in every corner and hole, search diligently, grope or feel, spy out, scout about, assay and prove, trace, trail, or follow by the track — these alone will not produce the result Dr. Eccles has achieved. There must be a directing imagination to guide the process, and a memory stored with rare Elizabethan things, some of which, rightly understood, can be made to dovetail in uncanny fashion with the new-found materials.

The present book contains a wealth of fresh matter to astonish and delight. Marlowe is the lodestone, the magnetic pole. Dr. Eccles, in adding a generous chapter to the poet's life, which confirms our notion of the violence of his character, has observed and deduced so shrewdly while following the compass course that he has discovered a new group of Marlowe's associates, led by the poet Thomas Watson. Watson, a great unknown in the complicated Elizabethan equation, emerges here for the first time in his habit as he lived. Dr. Eccles opens the door of the close chamber of literary history and influence within which too much of Elizabethan scholarship has been confined, and follows the companions Watson and Marlowe out into the intrigue, violence, and hurlyburly of Tudor London.

To our terror, he shows us the dramatists seconding each other in a fatal fight; in the sequel, he attends them to prison in Newgate; on Marlowe's release, he traces him to discover his lodging in London, and subsequently finds the poet and sworder there writing a Latin dedication to one of Watson's works, and threatening the parish constables with grievous bodily harm.

Watson on the other hand is traced back to his studies of the canon and civil law on the Continent; thence to the English College at Douai, and finally to his pardon for manslaughter in London, and some highly dubious proceedings as a professional wizard in the parish of St. Helen's, Bishopsgate, where Shakespeare was later a parishioner. If Shakespeare was indeed "Watsons heyre," we may hope that he refused at least the baser parts of the legacy.

But no tedious brief bill of fare is adequate to announce the rich and intricate feast provided by our author, to which every guest will hasten.

LESLIE HOTSON

CONTENTS

CHAPTER I

New Light on Marlowe

ON NO poet has keener interest centered in recent years than upon Marlowe. A succession of discoveries ever since the beginning of the century culminated in 1925 in that brilliant example of exploration in English archives, Professor Leslie Hotson's bringing to light the official record of Marlowe's death, and in his further identification of the dramatist as a confidential agent in affairs of state.[1] The new material flowing in from many sources has been admirably summarized in two books by scholars of sound judgment, *Marlowe and his Circle* (Oxford, 1929) by Dr. F. S. Boas, and *The Life of Marlowe* (London, 1930) by Professor Tucker Brooke. These works mark a stage in the progress of investigation, a plateau where we can conveniently find assembled all that is known. They by no means indicate that we have reached the peak of our knowledge and seen as far as it is possible to see. Rather, we are only at the beginning of the climb. In the Public Record Office and elsewhere there are forests of manuscripts whose recesses have never been explored, and here for generations searchers can continue to find buried treasure.

The life of Marlowe, if it could ever be written entire, would be as full of pity and terror as any of his plays. It is not to be wondered at that we desire to know more of

1. *The Death of Christopher Marlowe*, London and Cambridge, Mass., 1925.

the poet who mounted higher than any of the Elizabethans but one, who lived more swiftly and intensely than
any, and was struck down more suddenly. No man's
career could be more like the lightning in the collied night,
flashing forth, and then devoured by darkness: "So quick
bright things come to confusion." Marlowe's life, moreover, has the fascination of the unknown. Such fragments
of it as we do succeed in discovering only intensify the
silence and blackness of the rest. Of the six years of his
prime, nothing is known beyond a few casual allusions and
the charges made at the time of his arrest and death. Between the Privy Council's letter on his behalf to the University of Cambridge in 1587 and the warrant which it
issued in 1593 for his arrest, only one definite record of
Marlowe has been found. From this record we shall take
our start. The questions to which we seek an answer con-
cern his life during the years of his triumphs as the first
great English dramatist: Where did he live while he was
writing *Faustus* and the other plays? What poets among
his contemporaries were his friends and companions?
What breach of the law brought him in 1589 a prisoner
to Newgate?

By the bond into which he entered on October first of
that year Marlowe pledged himself to appear at the next
Sessions of Newgate to answer to all such matters as might
be objected against him. A document so vague and all-
embracing provokes our curiosity. "Most of his biographers," writes Miss Una Ellis-Fermor,[1] "agree that the
trouble was connected with the theatres, for the circumstances and form of the entry show that the offence was
committed within the City of London." The inference

1. *Christopher Marlowe* (1927), p. 5.

would not follow even if the premises were correct. They are not, for two distinct kinds of Sessions were held at Newgate, one for Middlesex as well as the other for London. Writers on this subject are generally only drawing upon the unreliable statements of J. H. Ingram in *Christopher Marlowe and his Associates* (1904).[1] Free rein is there given the imagination in picturing Marlowe's stout defiance of the Puritanical Lord Mayor, which made him liable to "all kinds of pains and penalties. He may have rendered himself suspected on account of the language of his *dramatis personae*, or he may have attempted to uphold the right of the actors to perform, and have even incited them to do so, in spite of the Lord Mayor's attempt to stay them." Since 1589 was the year of the merry wars of Marprelate, and since Lord Strange's company did disregard the Lord Mayor's orders by playing at the Cross Keys, Ingram's conjecture was tempting. None the less, it was not Marlowe's championship of the stage which brought about his arrest. Mr. Brooke comes closer to the true reason when he suggests,[2] having compared the usual causes which led to an Old Bailey recognizance, that Marlowe was bound over to keep the peace, like Master Downright in *Every Man in his Humour*.

After publishing *The Death of Christopher Marlowe*, Mr. Hotson for his further investigations chose this document as the most tantalizing bit of evidence in Marlowe's biography. He discussed it in *The Atlantic Monthly* for July, 1926, in an article entitled "Marlowe among the Churchwardens," summing up thus: "Christopher Marley, or Marlowe, then, is indicted for felony, and is ad-

1. Pp. 143–152.
2. *The Life of Marlowe*, p. 44 n.

mitted to bail. What was his offense? Was he convicted? Nobody knows." Since he was not able to discover anything about the recognizance itself, he traced the two sureties who gave bail for Marlowe, Richard Kitchen of Clifford's Inn, gentleman, and Humphrey Rowland of East Smithfield, horner, and found them in other records. He had in mind the possibility of being guided by them to Marlowe's address; but the result did not prove very enlightening. The recognizance was a riddle that refused to be solved, and where Marlowe lived in London remained unknown.

Marlowe must, however, have had other friends than the subsidy-men who went bail for him, or than the three men who happened to be at Deptford with him on the last day of his life, Ingram Frizer, Robert Poley, and Nicholas Skeres. He would not have been the poet we know in his plays if he had never associated with better company than this. His real familiars are likely to have been men who shared his love of poetry, such as Thomas Walsingham, or who were poets themselves. It occurred to me, therefore, that the best way to strike new sources of information about Marlowe might be to look up everything possible that concerned other university poets of the time who could be brought into relation with him. Kyd and Nashe are the best-known of his friends among the poets. I believed, however, that there would be more likelihood of finding something new about a less conspicuous author, such as Matthew Roydon, whom Kyd names as an acquaintance of Marlowe, or Thomas Watson.

Very few writers on Marlowe even mention the name of Watson, and yet it would be extremely strange if the two men had not known each other. Watson was not only the most admired Latin poet of his time in England. For his English verses he was ranked even by Gabriel Harvey with Sidney and Spenser. He was also one of the boon companions of the Bohemian group of university poets in London, as appears by the anecdote Nashe tells in *Have with You to Saffron Walden* (1596)[1] concerning "M. *Thomas Watson*, the Poet":

A man he was that I dearely lou'd and honor'd, and for all things hath left few his equalls in *England*, he it was that in the company of diuers Gentlemen one night at supper at the Nags head in *Cheape*; first told me of his vanitie, and those Hexameters made of him,

> *But o what newes of that good* Gabriell Haruey,
> *Knowne to the world for a foole and clapt in the Fleet*
> *for a Rimer.*

Shakespeare in 1595 seems to be called, for his *Venus and Adonis*, "Watsons heyre." [2] Peele in *The Honour of the Garter* names Watson among the great English poets now in heaven, in suggestive juxtaposition to his invocation of Marlowe immediately after.

Watson was a playwright as well, for his employer William Cornwallis wrote after his death that he "could devise twenty fictions and knaveryes in a play which was his daily practyse and his living." [3] No one knows which of the pre-Shakespearian plays he may have written, but they probably included both tragedies and comedies. For while Meres names Watson as one of the best for tragedy, the words of Cornwallis imply comedy, and the author of

1. Signatures T 3^v–4; R. B. McKerrow, *The Works of Thomas Nashe*, III (1905), 126 f.; cf. I (1904), 300.

2. William Covell, *Polimanteia*, sig. R 3; reprinted in A. B. Grosart, *Elizabethan England in Gentle and Simple Life* (1881), p. 45.

3. *The Athenæum*, August 23, 1890, p. 256 (not 1880, as in the *D.N.B.*).

Ulysses upon Ajax [1] speaks of Harington's etymologies as "the froth of witty Tom Watson's jests, I heard them in Paris fourteen years ago: besides what balductum play is not full of them?"

But there is a particular reason for associating Watson with Marlowe. In 1590 he dedicated his *Meliboeus* "Generosissimo Viro Thomæ Walsinghamo Armigero" — to the very man with whom Marlowe was living in 1593, the master of Ingram Frizer. Watson as Corydon carries on a dialogue with Walsingham as Tityrus, bemoaning the death of his cousin Sir Francis, and the verses show that Thomas Walsingham had known Watson in Paris many years before, and that the two were good friends. Marlowe, then, as a friend of Thomas Walsingham, would certainly know Thomas Watson. Accordingly, I engraved Watson in my mind as a man to be eagerly watched for, not for the sake of his own *Passionate Century of Love* or his *Tears of Fancy*, but as in all likelihood a companion of Marlowe.

This he proved in fact to have been. On the last day of a summer in London, I came upon a document which joins his name with that of "Christoferus Morley." It was four o'clock when I made the discovery; the Record Office closes at four twenty-five. There was no time lost in my reading to the end of those parchments. I shared the news at once with Mr. Hotson, who aided me in securing photostats of them; for my boat-train left at eight the next morning for Southampton, and this was my final day in England.

The documents are among the Chancery Miscellanea,

1. 1596, p. 15 (Harvard copy); in the British Museum copy the first phrase reads, "the froth of wittie *Iohn Watsons* idle iests."

Bundle 68, file 12, number 362, and consist of a writ and return into Chancery of a Gaol Delivery at Newgate, reciting the coroner's inquest. The Patent Rolls for 32 Elizabeth (part 4)[1] contain also a pardon, just as they do for Ingram Frizer. The story which these records have to tell follows.

I

On the afternoon of September 28, 1589, between two and three o'clock, William Bradley and "Christoferus Morley" of London, gentleman, were fighting together in Hog Lane. Thus abruptly does the framer of the indictment at the coroner's inquest the next day begin his tale. He says nothing about how the combat began, whether it was Marlowe or Bradley who gave the provocation, or whether the two men were enemies who fought on sight. Leaving all such matters to the imagination, he plunges, as Marlowe's companion was to do, into the midst of the fray.

The people in the street, seeing swords flashing, raised a clamor. Shakespeare, in *Romeo and Juliet* (I. i. 80), gives us the cry of the citizens at such a time: "Clubs, bills, and partisans! Strike! Beat them down!"

Thomas Watson of London, gentleman, was evidently close at hand. He drew his sword, like Romeo, to separate the two men, and to keep the Queen's peace. Such, at least, is the pacific motive with which the coroner's jury credits him. But Marlowe was more wary than Mercutio, or perhaps only more weary by now and ready to welcome a rest. Instead of risking a wound under his friend's arm, he drew back and ceased from fighting.

1. C 66/1340. The pardon is also recited in the Originalia, E 371/540, no. 71.

Bradley, however, was in no mood to stop. He saw Watson, with drawn sword, coming between him and his opponent, and instantly turned to meet his new enemy.

"Art thou now come?" he called out. "Then I will have a bout with thee." These, except for proper names, are the only English words in the record. They suggest that the quarrel was of more than a moment's standing: that the new enemy was also an old one.

At once Bradley flung himself on Watson and attacked him not only with his sword in one hand but also with a dagger in the other. With these weapons Bradley succeeded in cutting and wounding Watson so severely that his life was despaired of. Watson protected himself as best he could with his sword. To save himself he even retreated as far as a certain ditch in Hog Lane; but beyond this limit he could not flee without peril of his life.

Bradley, following up his advantage, pursued his adversary to continue the assault. Watson had no way of escape; and thereupon, for the saving of his own life, he struck Bradley a mortal blow. The sword entered the right breast near the nipple, making a wound an inch in breadth and six inches deep. Of this mortal blow, at Finsbury in the county of Middlesex, William Bradley instantly died.

There were at the time two coroners for Middlesex, Richard Vale and Ion Chalkhill,[1] gentlemen. The latter presided over the inquest at Finsbury on the following

---

1. See the *D.N.B.* under "Chalkhill, John," author of *Thealma and Clearchus* (1683). Because the title-page calls him "An Acquaintant and Friend of Edmund Spencer," the poet has hitherto been confused with the coroner, as in the *D.N.B.* and in George Saintsbury's *Minor Poets of the Caroline Period* (1906), II, 369. I shall show elsewhere that Ion Chalkhill had two sons, Ion and John, and that the younger, John, a Fellow of Winchester, was the poet.

day. He summoned a Middlesex jury to view the body of William Bradley, there lying slain, and to declare how he had come by his death. Marlowe and Watson, now in custody, were presumably present to give their evidence. The twelve jurymen were Geoffrey Witworth, William Vernon, William Yomans, Peter Pawson, Thomas Cowper, John Holmes, Thomas Kingeston, John Harlowe, Richard Owen, William White, William Homan, and John Hyde.

Was the third of these jurors, one wonders, the same William Yeomans, cutler, with whose wife Robert Poley had eloped less than a twelvemonth earlier? Yeomans testified before Recorder Fleetwood on January 7, 1588/9, that Poley, on being freed from the Tower by Walsingham about Michaelmas, had come to lodge with him, and, it was feared, to "beguile him either of his wyfe or of his lyfe." He finally preferred the first alternative. To that end he succeeded in getting his host imprisoned in the Marshalsea, where he himself as a prisoner some five years earlier had given "fyne Bankettes" to Yeomans' wife and refused to see his own — "one Watsons daughter." Her marriage to Poley cannot be traced in the parish registers, because, as Yeomans testified, it was performed secretly by a seminary priest in Bow Lane.[1] The juror is perhaps more likely to have been William Yeomans, tallow-chandler, constable of Shoreditch in 1586, a surety in 1590, and buried in January, 1590/91, from Church End, Shoreditch.[2] The foreman of the jury was "Jeofferey Whitworth, tallowchaundler," who with his wife Johan occupied

1. S. P. Dom. Eliz. 222/4, 13, 14; F. S. Boas, "Robert Poley: An Associate of Marlowe," *The Nineteenth Century and After*, October, 1928, pp. 543–552, and *Marlowe and his Circle*, pp. 31–34, 44, 54–55.
2. Middlesex Sessions Rolls 239/38, 245/39, 261/1, 270/24, 292/18, 293/36; register of St. Leonard's, Shoreditch.

in 1576 a house on the east side of Holywell Street, next to the Swan and the Bell.[1]

Another of the jurors, John Hyde, may conceivably have already been acquainted with Marlowe, if he was the John Hyde, citizen and grocer, who had been the legal owner of the Theater in Shoreditch since 1580, when James Burbage and John Brayne forfeited the mortgage he held upon it. Hyde's interest in the Theater was purely financial, but he had been brought into close relations with it through his efforts to recover his investment by arresting Burbage and by appointing an agent to take up a share of the daily receipts from plays. On June 7, 1589, three months before the inquest, he disposed of his title to the Theater to Cuthbert Burbage, and he later told the story of these dealings in Chancery.[2] Hyde, at least, would know something of the author of plays so successful as the two parts of *Tamburlaine*.

When the coroner's jury had heard the story of the fight in Hog Lane, it was their duty to decide whether Thomas Watson was guilty of either murder or manslaughter. Had he killed Bradley with malice aforethought or wilfully and feloniously? If their verdict was for either, he would have to come before the grand jury and hope to escape with a branding after reading his Latin neck-verse, as another excellent Latinist, Ben Jonson, was to do at Newgate just nine years later. They decided, however, that Watson had acted only in self-defense. He had slain Bradley against the Queen's peace, crown, and dignity, but not by felony nor in any other manner than was necessary to preserve

1. London County Council, *Survey of London*, VIII (1922), 11.
2. C. W. Wallace, *The First London Theatre, University of Nebraska Studies*, XIII (1913), 53–56, 106–112.

his own life. The coroner and each juror in turn affixed his seal to the verdict, and Marlowe and Watson could now breathe more freely as they marched from Finsbury to what they knew would be but a temporary imprisonment in Newgate. On October 1, 1589, Marlowe secured his freedom by giving a substantial bond, with two sureties, Richard Kitchen and Humphrey Rowland, for his appearance at the next Gaol Delivery.[1]

The brief and uncommunicative memorandum of this bond is the only document in the case which has been known up to the present time. Jeaffreson published it in 1886, but he did not recognize that it referred to Marlowe, because of the variant form in which the name appears, Christopher "Marley." This is the form under which Marlowe obtained his Master's degree, and which Peele used in his tribute in *The Honour of the Garter*, a month after the poet's death:

> *Marley*, the Muses darling for thy verse;
> Fitte to write passions for the soules below.

When Sir Sidney Lee wrote the life of Marlowe for the *Dictionary of National Biography*, seven years after the publication of the document, it was still unnoticed. In the following year he called attention to it in *The Athenæum*.[2] He interpreted the year "31 Elizabeth" as 1588, forgetting that Elizabeth did not come to the throne until late in the year 1558, on November 17, so that October of the thirty-first year of her reign was 1589. Mr. Ingram gave the date correctly underneath his facsimile of the record, but in his text (p. 143) he continued to refer to the

1. J. C. Jeaffreson, *Middlesex County Records*, I, 189; facsimile in J. H. Ingram, *Christopher Marlowe and his Associates*, p. 149.
2. August 18, 1894, pp. 235 f.

imprisonment as taking place "towards the close of 1588." The error was given currency in the revised edition of the *Dictionary of National Biography* and accordingly has misled many writers on Marlowe, even Sir Edmund Chambers in *The Elizabethan Stage* and Mr. Hotson in *The Death of Christopher Marlowe*, amended in *The Atlantic Monthly* for July, 1926.

By his recognizance Marlowe bound himself to appear in person at the next Sessions of Newgate to make answer to everything that might be objected against him on behalf of the Queen. Since the record was found among the Gaol Delivery Rolls, it appeared that the matters concerning which he was to answer constituted felony, but of what sort could until now be only conjectured. Our newly discovered documents have furnished definite information about what had happened to cause Marlowe's arrest. This is not the only question to which they supply an authoritative answer. They tell us further how long it was before Marlowe had to make his appearance at the Old Bailey, who were the justices he and Watson had to satisfy, and what went on at the hearing of the case.

II

The Gaol Delivery of Newgate at which Marlowe and Watson appeared was held at "Justice hall in Le Olde Bailie" on December 3 in the thirty-second year of Elizabeth (which had begun on November 17, 1589). On the bench sat the Lord Mayor of London, Sir John Harte; Chief Justices Wray of the Queen's Bench and Anderson of the Common Pleas; the Master of the Rolls, Sir Gilbert Gerrard, representing Chancery; Sir Roger Manwood,

Chief Baron of the Exchequer; Sir Rowland Heyward and Sir George Bond, Aldermen; Serjeant Fleetwood, Recorder of London; Robert Wroth, esquire; and others their fellow-justices assigned to the Gaol Delivery of prisoners in Newgate. The court was thus made up of three groups of justices: the great judges of the Crown, four in number; four City officials — the Lord Mayor, two former Lord Mayors, and the Recorder; and other Middlesex justices, such as Robert Wroth of Enfield. Because the Old Bailey is within the City of London, the Lord Mayor presided, but the Gaol Delivery was being held for the county of Middlesex, where Bradley had met his death.

The ranking officers of the Crown were Sir Christopher Wray and Sir Gilbert Gerrard, both of whom had close connections with the University of Cambridge. Gerrard had become counsel to the University in 1561, and the Senate wrote him a special letter of congratulation in 1581, when he became Master of the Rolls. Wray, also, received their grateful acknowledgment that it was his influence chiefly which secured for them the statute of 13 Elizabeth, c. 29, confirming the liberties and privileges of the University. Sir Christopher had not long since built or rebuilt three stories of Magdalene, his college, and is said to have erected the rich Renaissance west porch; he also founded fellowships and scholarships. Both he and Gerrard would probably have been well disposed towards a Cambridge Master of Arts.

Chief Justice Anderson, on the other hand, had a reputation for looking on prisoners "with a strange fierceness of countenance." Even his portrait would be proof that not the clearest conscience could make one feel at ease under that piercing, hawk-like eye. He had won his pro-

motion by the zeal with which he condemned Robert
Browne, on the Protestant side, and Edmund Campion,
on the Catholic, at trials where he "dismayed the prisoners" by his violent invective. "I pray you, let us make
short work with him," he bade his fellow-judges when the
Puritan writer John Udall came before the bar, and he
behaved with like harshness at the trials of Essex and of
Raleigh. It was fortunate for Marlowe that he appeared
at the Old Bailey only for a minor part in a case of justi-
fiable homicide and not for his opinions on religion. It
was on January 14, 1588/9, that Francis Kett, fellow of
Marlowe's own college, was burnt for heresy in the Castle
Ditch at Norwich.

All the Crown officers present on the bench had also
been employed earlier in the year, in April, at the arraignment of Philip Howard, Earl of Arundel, the first patron
of Watson. The chief justices had passed judgment on
Babington, Parry, and many others charged with high
treason, and with Manwood they were among the judges
who sentenced Mary Stuart at Fotheringay. Robert
Wroth, likewise, was frequently chosen as a commissioner
to try persons accused of treason: in 1586 the Babington
conspirators, in the spring of 1593 Jesuits and suspected
coiners, in the next reign Raleigh and the Gunpowder
plotters. He was father of the Sir Robert Wroth to whom
Jonson addressed the third epistle of *The Forest*, in praise
of country happiness, and who married Lady Mary Sidney,
dedicatee of *The Alchemist* and authoress of the Arcadian
romance *Urania*. Wroth is again named first among the
ordinary justices of Middlesex whom the Council required
in 1597 to take present order that no more plays should be
performed that summer within three miles of London.

The justices were directed to command the owners of the Curtain and the Theater "to plucke downe quite the stages, gallories and roomes" in such fashion that they might not be used again for the performance of plays.[1]

The City officials who sat at the December Gaol Delivery were particularly stout opponents of the public stage. Sir John Harte, in the zeal of his new office as Lord Mayor, which he had held only a week, wrote enthusiastically on November 6, 1589, that according to the Council's direction he had sent for all actors and had required them to forbear playing until further order. The Admiral's Men dutifully obeyed, but Lord Strange's company, for whom Marlowe may also at this time have been writing, very contemptuously went to the Cross Keys in Gracechurch Street and played that afternoon, whereupon Harte promptly committed some of them to one of the Counters. While still an alderman, Harte was one of a committee chosen on November 23, 1587, to repair to the Lords of the Council "to move theyre honours for the suppressinge of playes and interludes within this Cittye and the libertyes of the same." Sir George Bond was in his first month of office as Lord Mayor when this move was taken, and the head of the delegation was his fellow-justice on the present occasion, Sir Rowland Heyward.[2]

Heyward was especially influential as "the ancientest Alderman" of the City, brother-in-law of Sir Thomas Gresham, and one of the few men who have been twice elected Lord Mayor.[3] He often entertained Queen Elizabeth at his manor house of Hackney, which after his death

1. *Acts of the Privy Council of England, New Series*, XXVII (1903), 313 f.

2. E. K. Chambers, *The Elizabethan Stage* (1923), IV, 305.

3. J. J. Baddeley, *The Aldermen of Cripplegate Ward* (1900), p. 49; A. B. Beaven, *The Aldermen of the City of London*, II (1913), 172.

became the seat of the Earl of Oxford. Among the Chancery Town Depositions of 1578 we find Sir Rowland Heyward, aged sixty, deposing as to the will of Francis Langley's uncle, Sir John Langley. Last New Year's Day in the morning, Heyward relates, he had specially put Sir John in mind that in order to be buried according to his calling of alderman it would be necessary to raise three hundred pounds by selling houses in Cheapside. "Sʳ John Langley pawsed A litle/ and then answered, saying, Naked I came into the world, and naked I shall go out againe," and gave his consent. "Robert Crowley Preacher," the author, also signed a deposition, which fixes his age as sixty-one on October 3, 1578, telling how on that day he gave Langley ghostly counsel for his soul's health. The Dean of Paul's (Alexander Nowell) was likewise present, and Mr. Fox (John Foxe, the martyrologist) willed Sir John to think upon Christ and to "hold vpp his handes in token of his godlye meaning." In the course of very interesting and detailed testimony, Francis Langley, draper, aged thirty (Shakespeare's associate in 1596), told the story of the last hours of his uncle, who lay speechless while Lady Langley, her cousin Townsend the lawyer, and Sir Rowland Heyward, overseer of the will, waved others away from the room to confer in secret, and, Francis feared, altered the will in favor of Sir John's young wife against his nephews Thomas and especially Francis, who "so long hath serued him." [1]

Heyward and Fleetwood, "Leicester's mad Recorder," were often bracketed as special instruments of the Earl, and Fleetwood served as a link between the City and the

1. *Ex parte* Thomas Langley, defendant, v. Ursula Langley, plaintiff, C 24/134.

Court. The most active of all Middlesex justices, it was he who took Marlowe's recognizance and freed him on the bail of Kitchen and Rowland. He wrote verses for Lambarde's *Perambulation of Kent* in 1576 and for Chaloner's *De Republica Anglorum instauranda* three years later, and in the year in question, 1589, Thomas Newton eulogized his eloquence. His heart was in the duties which he described in *The Office of a Justice of the Peace*. No one was more enthusiastic than he in scouring the streets for suspicious characters and in putting down disturbances at the playhouses. The most vivid accounts we have of the minor turmoils of the time in London come from his letters to Burghley in the Lansdowne Manuscripts, accounts which he humorously described as "these trifling Newgacions." After recounting how he had lodged in Newgate the actors in two of the riots which had begun at the Theater, he wrote in 1584 that the City had obtained the Council's letter to suppress and pull down both the Theater and the Curtain, upon which he had summoned the players of the Queen and of Lord Arundel (Watson's patron). His summons, however, did not budge the "stubburne fellow" James Burbage. Fleetwood had to send the under-sheriff to arrest him, "and at his commyng he stowtted me owt very hastie," declaring that he was Hunsdon's man, and "to die for it he wold not be bound." When later in the year the Queen's players petitioned for liberty to act within the City, the corporation replied "in a mercilessly critical vein" concerning this running "from Gods seruice to the Deuells," reminded the players that but for serving the Queen they were by their profession rogues, and impaled them on the horns of the dilemma that "To play in plagetime is to encreasce the plage by infection: to play out of plagetime is to draw the plage by offendinges of God upon occasion of such playes." This answer, as Chambers well suggests, "may perhaps be ascribed to the malicious wit of Recorder Fleetwood." [1] In 1589 the Recorder made a report on the right of sanctuary for criminals in Paul's Churchyard, where Marlowe was so intimate with the stationers, according to Kyd, an intimacy which I take to be Harvey's reason for his allusions to Marlowe in "Gorgon, or the Wonderfull yeare": [2]

Weepe Powles, thy *Tamberlaine* voutsafes to dye.

· · · · · · · · · ·

Whose Corps on Powles, whose mind triumph'd on Kent.
· · · · · · the *Highest minde*
That ever haunted Powles, or hunted winde.

Of all the justices present, Sir Roger Manwood was the one with whom Marlowe was most likely to have been acquainted, for his country residence was the manor house of Hawe, in St. Stephen's, or Hackington, just outside Canterbury. When he died there on December 14, 1592, he had already built himself a magnificent monument in the church, and there, "like his grandsire cut in alabaster," he still sits in his robes as Chief Baron of the Exchequer, thoughtfully contemplating a very chilly-looking skeleton.[3] A Latin epitaph on his death has been preserved, "In Obitum Honoratissimi Viri, Rogeri Manwood, Militis, Quaestorii Reginalis Capitalis Baronis," subscribed with

---

1. *The Elizabethan Stage*, I, 292; IV, 297 ff.
2. *A New Letter of Notable Contents* (1593), in *The Works of Gabriel Harvey*, ed. A. B. Grosart, I (1884), 295–296. See Hale Moore, "Gabriel Harvey's References to Marlowe," *Studies in Philology*, XXIII (1926), 344, 351–354.
3. Figure in William Boys, *Collections for an History of Sandwich in Kent* (1792), p. 247.

Marlowe's name. Whether the verses are correctly attributed remains a question which calls for more careful discussion than it has yet received. Manwood had acquired
a well-deserved reputation for oppression and the taking
of bribes. In the same first week of December, 1589,
when he sat on the bench at the Newgate Gaol Delivery,
the Privy Council was requiring him to answer the charges
of Sir Thomas Perrot that he had been guilty of covinous
pleading and corrupt compact.[1] "Hark in thine ear:
change places; and, handy-dandy, which is the justice,
which is the thief? . . . Robes and furr'd gowns hide all."

Before this powerful bench of justices, then, Marlowe
appeared at the Old Bailey on December 3, 1589, for the
saving of his bond, and saw his companion Watson brought
into court after eleven weeks in the vaults of Newgate.
The case of Thomas Watson, late of London, gentleman,
being called, the sheriff of London and Middlesex led him
to the bar. The sheriffs at the time of Watson's arrest
were Hugh Offley, Prince Arthur in the archery shows at
Mile End and dedicatee of Greene's *The Spanish Mas-
querado*, and Richard Saltonstall, Governor of the Merchant Adventurers.[2] Richard Gourney, Master of the
Haberdashers' Company, and Stephen Soame, later
Lord Mayor, had been elected for 1589–1590 and were
the sheriffs now in office. To them, and to Sir John
Harte, now Lord Mayor, Greene dedicated his collection
of aphorisms called *The Royal Exchange*.

1. S. P. Dom. Eliz. 229/12, 230/24, 82; *Acts of the Privy Council*, XVIII
(1899), 262.
2. C. B. Millican in *The Review of English Studies*, VI(1930), 167, and *Spenser
and the Table Round* (Cambridge, Mass., 1931), pp. 55, 60–63, 175–176; T. W.
Baldwin, *William Shakespeare Adapts a Hanging* (Princeton, 1931), chapter
VII, "Master Sheriff Hugh Offley"; Leverett Saltonstall, *Ancestry and Descendants of Sir Richard Saltonstall* (Cambridge, Mass., 1897), p. 5.

For Marlowe's death, our principal authority is the record of the inquest returned into Chancery by the coroner of the Household, William Danby. For Bradley, instead of the coroner's record, we have the account of the Gaol Delivery, which carries the story one step farther. In the main it incorporates the finding of the inquest verbatim, leaving out only, like the pardons to both Frizer and Watson, the closing formulas in which the jury declare that the slayer did not take flight, and their knowledge or ignorance of the amount of his goods and chattels. When Watson came before the bar, the inquest was produced as containing all that was necessary to explain the cause of his arrest. To this stage, then, belongs the official record which we have thus far been following and which may now be quoted as a consecutive whole:

Deliberacio Gaole domine Regine de Newgate facta pro Comitatu Middlesex apud Justice hall in Le Olde Bailie in parochia Sancti Sepulchri London tercio die Decembris Anno Regni Elizabethe dei gracia Anglie ffrancie et hibernie Regine fidei defensoris &c Tricesimo secundo coram Johanne Harte Maiore predicte Ciuitatis London Christofero wraye Milite capitali Justiciario dicte domine Regine ad placita corone ipsa tenenda assignato, Gilberto Gerrard Milite Magistro Rotulorum Curie Cancellarie Edmundo Anderson Milite Capitali Justiciario dicte domine Regine de Banco, Rogero Manwood Milite Capitali barrone Scaccarij eiusdem domine Regine Rowlando Heyward Milite, Georgio Bonde Milite, Willelmo ffleetwood serviente ad legem Ac Recordatore Ciuitatis London et Roberto Wrothe Armigero et alijs socijs suis Justiciariis dicte domine Regine ad gaolam predictam de prisoneriis in eadem existentibus deliberandam assignatis

Thomas Watson nuper de London generosus captus pro eo quod indicatus fuit per quandam Inquisicionem indentatam captam apud ffynnesburie in Comitatu Middlesex xxix^mo die

Septembris Anno Regni Elizabethe dei gracia Anglie ffrancie
et hibernie Regine fidei defensoris &c xxxj° Coram Ivone
Chalkehill generoso vno Coronatorum dicti Comitatus Middlesex super visum Corporis Willelmi Bradley ibidem iacentis
mortui et interfecti per Sacramentum Galfridi Witworth willelmi vernon (?) Willelmi Yomans, Petri Pawson, Thome Cowper
Johannis Holmes, Thome Kingeston, Johannis Harlowe, Ricardi
Owen willelmi white, willelmi Homan et Johannis Hyde pro-
borum et legalium hominum de predicto Comitatu Middlesex
Qui dicunt super sacramentum suum quod Vbi prefatus willelmus Bradley et quidam Christoferus Morley nuper de London
generosus vicesimo octavo die Septembris Anno tricesimo
primo supradicto fuerunt insimul pugnantes in quadam venella
vocata hoglane in parochia Sancti Egidij extra Creplegate in predicto Comitatu Middlesex inter horas secundam et terciam post
meridiem eiusdem diei Ibi intervenit eisdem die et anno et
infra horas predictas quidam Thomas watson nuper de london
generosus super clamorem populi ibidem astantis [1] ad separan-
dum prefatos willelmum Bradley et Christoferum Morley sic
pugnantes et ad pacem dicte domine Regine conservandam Et
gladium suum eam ob causam tunc et ibidem extraxit Super
quo prefatus willelmus [2] Morley seipsum retraxit & a pugnando
desistit Et super hoc predictus willelmus Bradley videns eundem
Thomam watson sic intervenientem ibidem cum gladio suo
extracto dixit ei in his Anglicanis verbis sequentibus videlicet
(arte thowe nowe come then I will haue a boute wth thee) Et
instanter idem willelmus Bradley in prefatum Thomam watson
tunc et ibidem insultum fecit et cum vno gladio et vno pugione
de ferro et Calibi predictum Thomam watson tunc et ibidem
verberauit vulnerauit et maletractauit Ita quod de vita eius
desperabatur Racione cuius prefatus Thomas watson cum gladio
suo predicto de ferro et calibi precij iij^s iiij^d quem in manu sua
dextra tunc et ibidem habuit et tenuit seipsum contra predictum
Willelmum Bradley tunc et ibidem defendit et a predicto willelmo Bradley pro saluacione vite sue vsque ad quoddam fossatum in venella predicta fugit vltra quod quidem fossatum

---

1. Read *adstantis*.   2. Read *Christoferus*.

idem Thomas watson absque periculo vite sue fugere non potuit Et predictus willelmus Bradley insultum suum predictum continuando prefatum Thomam Watson tunc et ibidem recenter insecutus fuit Super quo predictus Thomas Watson pro saluacione vite sue predictum Willelmum Bradley cum gladio suo predicto tunc et ibidem percussit dans ei vnam plagam mortalem siue vulnus in et super dextram partem pectoris ipsius willelmi Bradley prope mamillam profunditatis sex policum et latitudinis vnius pollicis de qua quidem plaga mortali idem Willelmus Bradley apud ffynnesbury predictum in predicto Comitatu Middlesex instanter obijt Et sic Juratores predicti dicunt super sacramentum suum predictum quod predictus Thomas Watson seipsum defendendo prefatum Willelmum Bradley modo et forma predictis interfecit et occidit contra pacem dicte domine Regine Coronam et dignitatem suas et non per feloniam nec aliquo alio modo quam vt supradictum est In Cuius rei testimonium tam coronator quam Juratores predicti huic Inquisicioni sigilla sua alternatim apposuerunt Datum die et anno primis supradictis &c.

Que quidem Inquisicio predicti Coronatoris modo hic recordatur Et modo venit predictus Thomas Watson Coram prefatis Justiciariis per vicecomitem Comitatus predicti ad barram hic ductus in propria persona sua Ac visa Inquisicione predicta prefatus Thomas Watson per Justiciarios predictos remittitur prisone in Custodia dicti vicecomitis ad graciam domine Regine expectandam.

Clerke.

The justices, then, found no reason to doubt the correctness of the verdict that Watson had killed Bradley in self-defense. They remanded him to Newgate to await the grace of the Queen, and his setting at liberty was now merely a matter of time and money. He was not so successful in securing a speedy release, however, as Ingram Frizer. After killing Marlowe on May 30, 1593, Frizer obtained the Queen's pardon only thirteen days later, on June 12. Watson had to wait until February 10, 1589/90, two months after his hearing in court, and nearly five months after he first entered "that infamous Castle of Misery," as Luke Hutton called it in *The Black Dog of Newgate*,

> Where was no day, for there was ever night. . .
> Robbed of the sky, the stars, the day, the sun.

The pardon, which also recites the coroner's inquest, runs as follows:

B*illa* p*er*don*e* se defendend*o* p*ro* Tho. Watson Regina Omn*i*b*us* Balliuis & fidelib*us* suis ad quos &c' sal*ute*m. Quia accepim*us* p*er* tenorem recordi & p*ro*cessus cuiusdam Inquisic*ion*is indentat*e* capt*e* apud ffynesburye in Com*itatu* midd*l*esex vicesimo nono die Septembris Anno regni n*ost*ri tricesimo primo coram Iuone Chalkehill Gen*er*oso vno Coronat*orum* d*ic*ti Com*i*tat*us* midd*l*esex sup*er* visum corporis Will*el*mi Bradley ibidem iace*nt*is mortui & int*er*fecti Q*uod* vbi p*re*fat*us* Will*el*m*us* Bradley & quidam Cristoferus morley nup*er* de london Gen*er*osus vicesimo octauo die Septembris Anno regni n*ost*ri tricesimo primo sup*radicto* fuerunt insimul pugnantes in quadam venella vocat*a* hoggelane in parochia *sancti* Egidij ext*ra* Crepulgate in p*re*dic*to* Com*itatu* midd*l*esex int*er* horas sec*un*dam & t*er*ciam post meridiem eiusdem diei ibi int*er*uenit eisdem die & Anno & infra horas p*re*dict*as* quidam Thomas Watson nup*er* de london Gen*er*osus sup*er* clamorem populi ibidem adstant*is* ad sep*ar*and*um* p*re*fat*os* Will*el*mu*m* Bradley & Cristoferum morley sic pugnantes & ad pacem n*ost*ram conseruand*am* Et gladiu*m* suu*m* eam ob causam tunc & ibidem ext*r*axit Sup*er* quo p*re*fatus Will*el*m*u*s morley seips*u*m retr*a*xit & a pugnando desistit Et sup*er* hoc p*re*dic*tu*s Will*el*m*u*s Bradley videns eundem Thomam Watson sic int*er*uenien*tem* ibidem cum gladio suo ext*r*acto dixit ei in hijs anglicanis v*er*bis seque*ntibus* videl*icet* Art thowe nowe come Then I will haue a boute with the Et instant*er* idem Will*el*mu*s* Bradley in p*re*fat*um* Thomam Watson tunc & ibidem insult*um* fecit & cum vno gladio & vno pugione de ferro & Calibe p*re*dic*tu*m Thomam Watson tunc & ibidem v*er*b*er*auit vulner-auit & male t*r*actauit Ita q*uod* de vita eius desp*er*abatur r*a*cione cuius p*re*fat*us* Thomas Watson cum gladio suo p*re*dic*to*

de ferro & chalibe precij trium solidorum quatuor denariorum
quem in manu sua dextra tunc & ibidem habuit & tenuit seipsum
contra predictum Willelmum Bradley tunc & ibidem defendidit
& a predicto Willelmo Bradley pro saluacione vite sue vsque
ad quoddam fossatum in venella predicta fugijt vltra quodqui-
dem fossatum idem Thomas Watson absque periculo vite sue
fugere non potuit. Et predictus Willelmus Bradley insultum
suum predictum continuando prefatum Thomam Watson tunc
& ibidem recenter insecutus fuit Super quo predictus Thomas
Watson pro saluacione vite sue predictum Willelmum Bradley
cum gladio suo predicto tunc & ibidem percussit dans ei vnam
plagam mortalem siue vulnus in & super dextram partem pectoris
ipsius Willelmi Bradley prope mamillam profunditatis sex
pollicum & latitudinis vnius pollicis de qua quidem plaga
mortali idem Willelmus Bradley apud ffynesburye predictam
in predicto Comitatu middlesex instanter obijt Et sic predictus
Thomas Watson seipsum defendendo prefatum Willelmum
Bradley modo & forma predictis interficit & occidit contra
pacem nostram & non per feloniam nec aliquo alio modo quam
vt supradictum est prout per tenorem recordi Inquisicionis
predicte nobis in Cancellariam nostram de mandato nostro
missam & in filacijs ibidem de recordo residentem plene liquet.
Nos pietate moti perdonauimus eidem Thome Watson sectam
pacis nostre que ad nos versus ipsum pertinet pro morte predicta
Et firmam pacem nostram ei inde damus & concedimus per
presentes Ita tamen quod stet recto in Curia nostra si quis
versus eum loqui voluerit de morte supradicta In cuius rei &c'.
Teste Regina apud Westm' x die ffebruarij.

III

To understand these documents, it is necessary to compare them with others of the same kind, and in this way
to discover what was the customary method of procedure.
The records that survive date sometimes from one stage
of a case, sometimes from another, and it is only by piec-
ing together what we can learn from corresponding trials

for homicide that a continuous story emerges. For example, we have no trace of an indictment against Watson, yet in a closely similar instance the indictment has been preserved, with notes of the prisoner's answer at his arraignment and later of his production of a pardon. The case of this prisoner, Charles Wren, offers an especially good parallel, inasmuch as he, like Watson, came before the bench at a Gaol Delivery in 1589. His trial was in fact the most recent example at that time of a prosecution for homicide in Middlesex.

Charles Wren was of a good family in Durham — he lived to be knighted in 1607. The Wrens were known among their neighbors by an epithet as significant as it is amusing: they were called the "Wrathful Wrens" of Binchester.[1] Charles, the eldest son and heir, evidently inherited his rightful share of the family wrath. Of the same age as Marlowe, being eleven in 1575 when he matriculated at Brasenose, he entered Gray's Inn in 1583/4. His victim, Robert Radcliffe, was evidently the Robert of Sturmer, Essex, who was also of Gray's Inn, a kinsman to the Earl of Sussex.[2] Charles Wren of Gray's Inn, according to the story told at the coroner's inquest, between eleven and twelve in the morning of January 21, 1588/9, was walking in the fields from Gray's Inn towards "Marybone Park." Seeing Wren, Radcliffe followed and met him on his way back "in quadam venella voc*ata* lustie lane alias longe lane apud Maribone." There he demanded the payment of ten pounds which he claimed Wren owed him. A quarrel followed; Radcliffe drew sword and dagger

1. J. C. Hodgson, *North Country Diaries* (*Second Series*), Surtees Society, CXXIV (1915), 205 f.
2. Joseph Foster, *The Register of Admissions to Gray's Inn* (1889), p. 62.

and made an assault on Wren, who also drew, and in the fray plunged his sword into the other's right breast — a mortal blow of which Radcliffe then and there, at "Marybone Park," died instantly. This, we must remember, is the survivor's account of the affair. It is quite possible, on the other hand, that there had been a regular challenge to a duel in an unfrequented country lane. Marylebone Park remained a favorite dueling-ground throughout the eighteenth century. Here Sir Charles Blount began his friendship with Essex by wounding him in the thigh, and the author of *Ulysses upon Ajax* [1] writes of "that great stile into *Maribone* Parke, neer which the two Heroicall and manly Knights fought there *Duellum*." The coroner's jury did not investigate Radcliffe's death until more than a month later, on February 26, and they then accepted Wren's statements that he drew his weapons only to save his life and endeavored to retire, but that his assailant, attacking him "furiose et violenter," resolutely forced the fray upon him.

The value of Wren's case as an illustration is that we have concerning it, among the Chancery Miscellanea, all the documents such as are preserved for Watson, and also, at the Middlesex Guildhall, both the coroner's inquest and the indictment. [2] The completeness of the record gives us an excellent opportunity to follow the procedure that Watson likewise went through. In the first place, after the inquest Wren was indicted at a Session of the Peace held at the Castle in St. John Street (the tavern used

1. 1596, sig. D 1; Sir Robert Naunton, *Fragmenta Regalia*, ed. Arber (1870), pp. 52–53.

2. These two are summarized by Jeaffreson, *Middlesex County Records*, I, 182–184. I have used the original documents, Sessions Roll 282, nos. 12 and 22, and added the information from Chancery Miscellanea 68/271.

for Sessions business) on April 11, 1589, before four justices for Middlesex. Next, he was arraigned at the Gaol Delivery of Newgate, led to the bar, and asked how he wished to clear himself — "qualiter se velit de felonia p^rdicta acquietare." In reply, "dicit quod ipse in nullo est Culpabilis Et de hoc de bono et malo ponit se super patriam." The clerk in his notes on the indictment puts the same thing in different words: he says that the prisoner "ponit se non culpabilem de felonia interfeccione," or "manslater," but guilty of killing Radcliffe in self-defense. The jury accepted the plea and returned a verdict to that effect. A writ was issued on April 28, declaring that Wren had killed Radcliffe *se defendendo*, not by felony nor with malice aforethought, and that he awaited pardon. He secured it on May 3 and at the Gaol Delivery of May 14 produced it before the court, thus obtaining his freedom. The memorandum on the grand jury's indictment of Wren — one of the jurymen on the panel was a Robert Marlowe [1] — and the full record of the Gaol Delivery together supply several steps necessary to reconstruct Watson's progress through the Old Bailey.

The only other case of homicide known to have occurred in the Middlesex suburbs of London in 1589 was the killing of Nicholas Fawcett by Sidrake Vere of London, gentleman, on January 8. The two men met "in publica platea" in St. John Street, and because of "diuersa opbrobria & contumeliosa verba" spoken by each in turn they drew swords and daggers and made an affray, in which Vere wounded Fawcett incurably so that he died a week later. As with Bradley, the wound was on the breast near the right nipple, but it was only three inches deep. Jeaffreson

1. Sessions Roll 281, no. 16.

adds,[1] "The unusual length of the time between the fatal result and the date of the inquest [February 7] is note-worthy"; but he overlooks the fact that above the name of Vere in the original inquest appear the words "extra prisonam." The "manqueller" had escaped arrest, and the coroner probably waited for a time to see whether he would be apprehended. Even so the interval was shorter than that before the inquest on Radcliffe. Since Vere was not present to explain how reluctant he had been to kill his opponent, there is no allegation of self-defense in the verdict, which must have been founded upon the testimony of eye-witnesses and, possibly, of the victim himself during the week he languished of the wound. There were witnesses also to the fray between Marlowe and Bradley, since it was "upon the clamor of the people" that Watson came to part the strife. What happened to Sidrake Vere I do not know, but if he escaped to Ireland or the Continent he lost a good income provided for him in England. For the Earl of Arundel, when he made his will as a prisoner in the Tower on June 12, 1588, bade his trustees allow "to my loving Servant Sidracke Vere for his Mayntenaunce till he come to possesse either the keping of the great parke at Arundell, or the Old parke at Keninghale, whereof he hath a patent in reversion of my guyft." Lord William Howard mentioned Vere in 1585 as one of the followers of the Earl, his brother, who in that year had joined in the Earl's secret attempt to fly beyond the sea.[2]

Of the three ways by which, in Elizabeth's time, one might kill a man and yet escape hanging, Watson and

1. *Middlesex County Records*, I, 182 f.; cf. Sessions Roll 282, no. 23.
2. *The Ven. Philip Howard, Earl of Arundel, 1557–1595*, Catholic Record Society, XXI (1919), 119, 377.

Wren got off by pleading self-defense and suing a pardon, Vere by flight, and Ben Jonson by benefit of clergy. The memorandum on the indictment against Jonson, "petit librum legit ut Clericus signatur cum litera T Et deliberatur," shows what happened when the prisoner could not plead self-defense and had to put himself guilty of manslaughter. Watson avoided being branded with the Tyburn "T" by satisfying the coroner's jury that he had not slain Bradley "feloniously and wilfully," as Jonson was declared by the indictment to have killed Gabriel Spencer.

CHAPTER II

In Newgate

THE story of the fray in Hog Lane has emerged from the newly discovered documents in so much detail that it is possible to form a clear picture of the actual combat. As with Marlowe's death in the tavern at Deptford, however, the coroner's inquest, instead of thoroughly satisfying our curiosity, only arouses it. In both instances the Chancery Miscellanea and the pardons on the Patent Rolls must remain our chief sources of information. Nevertheless, for the Bradley case, at least, they need not be our only sources. What happened to Marlowe and Watson after the slaying of Bradley and the inquest on his body in September, 1589, but before the signing of the pardon in February following? This should be a matter of record elsewhere than in Chancery.

Even the one bit of evidence that has been known, Marlowe's recognizance, has not been made to yield all that it has to tell. Sir Sidney Lee cited only the brief abstract given by Jeaffreson. J. H. Ingram published a useful facsimile of the record, but paid no attention to a memorandum which appears in the margin; nor did Mr. Hotson or Dr. Boas when they in turn translated and discussed the document. Mr. Brooke in his recent *Life of Marlowe*,[1] though sending the reader three years out

1. Pp. 96–97, citing "*Athenæum*, 18 Aug. 1897," where the year should be "1894."

of the way in his reference to Lee, has printed an expansion
of the Latin which is very satisfactory, except for the note
in the margin which he transcribes "'recd & del & proclam.'" He does not offer any explanation of its meaning;
but, as a matter of fact, an examination of the reproduction
in Ingram shows that the correct reading of the memorandum is "reu' & del' per proclam'." When expanded, it
will therefore read, "reu*ertitur et* del*iberatur* per procla-
m*acionem.*" The clerk added the annotation at a later
date, of course, to show that the recognizance was no
longer in force. From this overlooked note, then, we learn
that Marlowe kept his pledge to present himself again at
Newgate, so that Kitchen and Rowland lost nothing
through their suretyship for him; and that he was discharged by the justices there, or in Elizabethan phrase,
"quit by proclamation."

So much for the recognizance. But what of Marlowe's
imprisonment in Newgate? At first there seemed little
hope of finding anything about it after so many years of
interest in the subject on the part of skilled biographers.
The comments of scholars were uniformly discouraging:
Lee, for example, remarked that the charge against Marlowe "is unfortunately not stated, and I am not sure that
the investigation can be carried further." And Mr.
Hotson wrote in *The Atlantic Monthly* for July, 1926, "It
was tantalizing to find that there seemed to be no possibility of further light on the case. A search among the
remaining records of the Middlesex Sessions afforded
nothing."

Nevertheless, it is always well to see for one's self, and
I resolved to do so, though I could hardly expect to come
upon anything of value where the most distinguished of

record-searchers had reported no success. The Sessions records are not kept at the Public Record Office, but still remain, excellently cared for, in the custody of the county at the Middlesex Guildhall, opposite Westminster Abbey and facing the Houses of Parliament. I had already become fairly familiar with the records there in hunting the trail of poets in the reign of James I. The summer after my first meeting with William Bradley, therefore, I stopped in at the Middlesex Guildhall as a matter of form, and looked up the files for 1589. The quarry I found surprised me, and made it evident that no one had ever gone hunting here for Marlowe, despite the fact that the recognizance which Jeaffreson happened by accident to publish marked it out as the most likely covert. Marlowe's biographers from Lee to Brooke had rested content with the single record, and it turned out that even Mr. Hotson had never himself been at the Middlesex Guildhall and was apparently trusting to Ingram's statement that "the Roll contains nothing further."

Marlowe's recognizance, the first item in Sessions Roll 284, is followed by a list of jurors, including one named William Kempe, by a presentment of Sir John Arundell and others as recusants, and by a number of indictments for robbery. The parchment which attracted my attention, however, was the twelfth and last, for there in a calendar of names stood out the following:

Thomas Watson nup*er* de Norton ffowlgate in Comi-*tatu* Midd*lesex* generos*us* & *Christ*oferus Marlowe nup*er* de Eadem yoman q*ui* duct*i* fuer*unt* Gaole xviij° die Septembris *per* Stephanu*m* wyld Const*abularium* ib*ide*m pro *S*uspicione Murdri viz *p*ro Morte (blank) et Com*m*iss*i* fuer*unt* per Owinu*m* Hopton Mil*item*

In the margin before Watson's name the memorandum has been added, "balliat*us*," and before Marlowe's, "del*iberatus* p*er* proclam*acionem*."

The list in which this entry appears is a sort of matriculation register of the prisoners in Newgate. It names the first new arrival on September 9, 1589, and was drawn up on October 2. There are twenty-six names in all, of which two are deleted, leaving an exact average of one person every day committed on suspicion of felony. Marlowe and Watson, we now discover, were arrested on a charge of murder, just as John Day was first arraigned on the charge of murdering his fellow-playwright Henry Porter in 1599 and later secured the modification of the indictment to manslaughter.[1]

The most surprising feature of the foregoing record is its date. According to the coroner's inquest, as quoted in later documents, the fray occurred on September 28, 1589. Yet here is a document made at Newgate itself stating that Marlowe and Watson were led to gaol on September 18. Where official records disagree, it is not easy to decide between them. Of the two, the coroner's inquest carried the greater authority, since it was to serve as a basis for legal proceedings, and it should have been the more carefully prepared. On the other hand, we must remember that we do not have the original inquest, but only copies of the greater part of it in the record of the Gaol Delivery and in the pardon. What has happened is evidently one of two alternatives: either these documents have transformed "xviij" into "xxviij," or the prison list at Newgate has made the opposite error. The list,

1. Hotson, "The Adventure of the Single Rapier," *The Atlantic Monthly*, July, 1931, pp. 26–31.

however, seems to be an original, and for the most part
the names of prisoners brought in are arranged in regular
chronological order. Watson and Marlowe come before
"Lucas Marshall nup*er* de Mile End in Com*itatu* Mid-
d*lesex* Spinster," who was arrested on September 20. The
Sessions Roll entry, therefore, inspires more confidence
than the official Chancery records, since it was written
down at the time instead of being copied more than two
months later. The question is settled in its favor by the
discovery of the parish register containing the record of
William Bradley's burial. As we shall see in the next
chapter, Bradley was buried on September 19, 1589. The
Chancery date of September 28 for the affray is thus a
manifest error. Since the coroner's jury gave its verdict on view of the body of William Bradley, the inquest
must likewise have preceded the burial, and the Chancery
date of September 29 for the inquest is an error for September 19.

According to the Newgate calendar, as we may ap-
propriately call it, Marlowe spent thirteen days in gaol
instead of three. He had thus an excellent opportunity
of becoming acquainted with the prisoners in Newgate,
both through his own stay and through coming later to
visit Watson. This fact is interesting in connection with
the accusation of Richard Baines in 1593 that Marlowe
had declared,

That he had as good Right to Coine as the Queen of England.
and that he was aquainted wth one Poole a prisoner in newgate
who hath great Skill in mixture of mettals and having learned
some thing*es* of him he ment through help of a Cunni*n*g stamp
maker to Coin ffrench Crownes pistolet*es* and English shilling*es*.[1]

1. Harleian MS. 6848, f. 185^v.

Mr. Brooke remarks, "This charge is scored through in the copy of the document made for official use, doubtless as irrelevant or obviously silly." [1] To consider a charge against Marlowe of counterfeiting as obviously silly may be natural to the admirer of his poetry, but it was not likely to be the attitude of Elizabethan officials, whose duty was to punish coining as petty treason, and who as a matter of course examined prisoners at the same time on coining and on religion.[2] There must have been other reasons for the deletion, and a possible cause might be suggested as unwillingness on the part of the Government to press a charge which would necessarily endanger the liberty, if not the neck, of a useful Government agent, supposing that "one Poole" was indeed "Ro*ber*te Poole al*ia*s Polley." As Dr. Boas observes, "If the identification is correct, Baines's allegation is of considerable importance, as the only link, outside of the legal records, between Marlowe and any of the three companions of his last hours, Robert Poley, Ingram Frizer, and Nicholas Skeres." [3] I do not think, however, that Poole is likely to have been Poley, since there is nothing to show that Poley was ever in Newgate, and since he cannot have been there at the time Baines wrote. Mr. Brooke may be right in his alternative suggestion that the coining charge was merely regarded as out of place among accusations of atheism. It was in Newgate, at any rate, and possibly, though not necessarily, in 1589, that Marlowe met the

1. *The Life of Marlowe*, p. 62 n.
2. See the examination of John Greene, coiner, with the order to arrest Ingram Greene of the Whitefriars, gent., and other coiners and Catholics on his evidence (*The Ven. Philip Howard, Earl of Arundel, 1557-1595*, Catholic Record Society, XXI [1919], 162).
3. *Marlowe and his Circle*, p. 31.

Mephistophilis who taught him how he might fill his purse with crowns and pistolets; as Faustus, when he imagined what desperate enterprises his spirits should perform, planned first of all to have them fly to India for gold.

The keeper of Newgate from 1580 to 1594 was William Deyos, succeeding a keeper who was removed on bitter complaint that "Crowder and his wife be most horrible blasphemers and swearers" and takers of bribes.[1] It is not necessary to suppose [2] that Deyos was a Spaniard, merely on account of his surname, especially if we consider that the Spaniards were not much beloved by the English at this time. The State Papers contain two records dealing with Newgate in the year of Marlowe's imprisonment: one, the examination of Robert Bellamy, of Harrow, about his escape from Newgate to Scotland and so over the sea to Hamburg; the other, a petition of the poor prisoners in Newgate to the Lord Admiral.[3] It was the common practise in time of war to free debtors and others in prison for minor offenses in order to enlist them as recruits, and the Admiral had evidently just been raising a levy of this sort in London. The Newgate petitioners tell him how gladly they also will enter the Queen's service if only he will change his writ so that it will allow the enlistment of persons who are not bailable by law. Marlowe, of course, was able to secure bail, and had no desire, therefore, to serve the Lord Admiral by sea, instead of by writing for the Admiral's Men at the Theater.

Let us reconstruct what happened to the two poets from

1. S. P. Dom. Eliz. 165/5; W. H. and H. C. Overall, *Analytical Index to the Series of Records Known as the Remembrancia* (1878), pp. 188 f., 284.

2. As in Arthur Griffiths, *The Chronicles of Newgate* (1884), I, 90. Cf. Roger Dyos or Deyos, the vicar of Stratford who christened Shakespeare's sister Joan.

3. S. P. Dom. Eliz. 228/31, 229/84.

the time Bradley fell mortally wounded. They would be charged to stay and abide the course of the law; the constable of the precinct, Stephen Wyld, tailor, would arrive on the scene and march them off to the nearest justice. This was Sir Owen Hopton, lieutenant of the Tower, then living in Norton Folgate, the Queen's kinsman by descent from Owen Tudor. For two years after the Babington plot in 1586, he had had Robert Poley in his keeping. In the month of September, 1589, when he issued the warrant to send Marlowe to Newgate, the most recent arrivals to come into his custody at the Tower were Lodowick Greville, the Warwickshire squire who, after strangling a neighbor, procured the murder of his servant for boasting at a drinking-match at Stratford that he knew what would hang his master — a fate which Greville avoided only by standing mute and dying by the *peine forte et dure*; and John Hodgkins, the chief printer of the Martin Marprelate tracts, who despite the rack told nothing of their authorship.[1]

Marlowe and Watson would next be led across the City to Newgate, and their names enrolled in the Black Book. Every new prisoner for felony was at first manacled and put in the dungeon called Limbo, the condemned hold between the top and bottom of the arch under Newgate. Most men supposed it to be underground, because it was "a dark Opace wild Room," entered by a hatch from above. No light illumined it but a candle set on a black stone, against which a desperate condemned man, the story ran, once dashed out his brains. This stone was the

1. S. P. Dom. Eliz. 227/37; C. C. Stopes, *Shakespeare's Warwickshire Contemporaries* (1907), pp. 162 ff.; William Pierce, *An Historical Introduction to the Marprelate Tracts* (1908), p. 197.

Black Dog of Newgate, according to one explanation given in *The Discovery of a London Monster* (1638). Another legend told of a scholar committed in the reign of Henry III for "charms and devilish witchcrafts," "which scholar, maugre his Devils, Furies, sprites and goblins, was by the famished prisoners eaten up," and who thereupon haunted them in the likeness of a hound. *The Black Dog of Newgate* was the title of a play written in 1602/3 by John Day, Richard Hathway, Wentworth Smith, and another, both parts of which are lost. But by good fortune the pamphlet of that name written by Luke Hutton gives a vivid account in verse of his first impressions of Newgate, which he entered in 1589, only a few months before Marlowe and Watson.

The verses bear witness to the author's personal experience of the prison by such passages as that which tells how "A rat doth rob the candle from my hands," while a hundred other rats sally forth in the pitch-darkness; or how he listens to the pitiful noise of a man in clanking irons, "Begging one penny to buy a hundred bread." When Limbo had worked its terrors upon the new prisoner, a gaoler came to daunt his spirits still more by further threats, "Swearing an oath that I did lie too soft,/ Who lay on ground, and thus at me he scoffed." He then demanded his garnish, or fee, in return for which he would strike off the man's leg-bolts, and give him his choice of lodging in the master's or the common side, according to the weight of his purse:

> If thou have any coin
> To pay for ease, I will a little wink,
>   And bolts' releasement with discharge I'll join
> Of this close prison to some other ward,
> Paying thy fine, or else all ease is barred. . . .

His mouth to stop, angels I gave him two,
Yielding perforce, as I perforce must do.

A new prisoner chose the master's side if he could possibly afford it, and since Marlowe expected to be soon out on bail, he would be able, if his own money ran short, to raise enough from friends for his short stay. Here on the master-felons' side the chief pastime was drinking in a vaulted cellar, called in a later pamphlet "the Boozing Ken." The novice pledged the whole company in wine; and, what with drinking and with paying the exorbitant fees the gaolers exacted, he generally came very quickly to the bottom of his purse, whereupon he was cast down into one of the lowest wards. Newgate had a bad reputation for gaol fever in Elizabeth's time; but since Marlowe was shortly released, and Watson seems to have had enough money to secure his pardon, they probably escaped the crowded Middle Ward and the underground Stone Hold.[1]

The results of killing a man in a duel are concisely described by one of Shirley's characters, Rawbone the usurer.[2] "I doe imagine my selfe apprehended already," he soliloquizes; "now the Constable is carrying me to Newgate — now, now, I'me at the Sessions house, i 'th Docke: — now I'me cald — not guilty my Lord: — the Iury has found the Inditement *Billa vera* — now, now comes my sentence."

To sum up the order of events: on September 18, 1589, Watson and Marlowe were arrested for the murder of William Bradley in Hog Lane. The constable of Norton

1. Arthur Griffiths, *The Chronicles of Newgate*; Charles Gordon, *The Old Bailey and Newgate* (1902); *The Black Dog of Newgate*, in A. V. Judges, *The Elizabethan Underworld* (1930).
2. James Shirley, *The Wedding* (1633), IV, i, sig. G 3ᵛ.

Folgate led them to the lieutenant of the Tower, who committed them to Newgate. On September 19 the coroner, Ion Chalkhill, held an inquest upon Bradley, and the jury found that Watson had killed him in self-defense. Marlowe could now be admitted to bail, and on October 1 he offered as sureties Humphrey Rowland, horner, and Richard Kitchen, an attorney of Clifford's Inn. He was freed on signing a recognizance in the large sum of forty pounds, binding himself to appear at the Old Bailey when called upon to answer. He kept his promise, appearing probably at the Gaol Delivery of December 3, when the justices for Middlesex heard the coroner's inquisition read and remanded Watson to prison to await the Queen's mercy. The royal pardon granted on February 12 following gave Watson the span of life which remained to him, which proved to be only two and a half years. During that brief time he lived at Bishopsgate as tutor to the son of William Cornwallis, and continued to "devise twenty fictions and knaveryes in a play which was his daily practyse and his living."

CHAPTER III

William Bradley

ONE question remains to be answered: Who was
William Bradley? The records introduce us to
him in the midst of his combat with Marlowe;
they describe his assault on Watson, and quote
some of his last words; but after Watson with "bloody
blameful blade" (price 3s. 4d.) had bravely broached
Bradley's boiling bloody breast, we hear no more of him
except as a corpse at the inquest. The only description
we have of him, therefore, is as the body "Willelmi Bradley ibidem iacentis mortui et interfecti" — not even "late
of London," as Marlowe was called, or "gentleman" or
"yeoman," since he was neither now. The problem before
us is to decide which of the many contemporary William
Bradleys he may have been.

The first William Bradley in the calendars of Chancery
proceedings who naturally attracts one's curiosity figures
in a suit of which the printed list tells us merely that the
plaintiff was "Bradley, William," the defendant "Pooley,
Robert," the cause of suit "Money matters," and the
county mentioned "Warwick." [1] It turns out, on examination of the pleadings, that besides Robert Poley, the spy
of Walsingham, there was another of the name, a baker
of Higham Ferrers, a man, according to Bradley, of no
more conscience than Marlowe's companion. He had

1. Public Record Office, *Lists and Indexes*, XXIV, 8: C 3/205/85.

arrested one Robert Hayes for a small debt and lodged him
in prison at Coventry, and on hearing that his debtor
had been released for a short time at Christmas, went to
Coventry and secured judgment against him. Bradley,
"being assured that the saide Hayes wold yeld his bodye
to the saide pryson," gave bond jointly with the keeper
of the prison, Ralph Vernon, that "yf he could not procure
the body of the said Hayes to be in execution before
Easter" he would pay Pooley the amount of the debt,
three pounds, at Coventry Fair. Imprisoned again in Lent,
Hayes has offered divers times to satisfy the debt, but
Pooley keeps him in gaol, utterly refuses to deliver the
bond, and threatens to sue Bradley at common law. Instead of answering, Pooley merely demurs that the court
of Chancery "doth not vse to hold plee or Jurisdiccion of
causes of so smale a value." Bradley's bill is signed by his
counsel "Marstone" — John Marston of Coventry, father
of John Marston the dramatist. The William Bradley in
this case was probably a Warwickshire attorney, the same
who appears as defendant to Edward Stonardes in a Chancery suit concerning property in Nuneaton and Chilvers
Coton, and as defendant to Thomas Eyborne in another
Coventry case.[1] In Trinity Term, 1588, William Bradley
joined with Thomas Somerfeild and others in suing for
perjury Thomas Whittingham of Thornbury, Gloucester,
yeoman.[2] Mr. Hotson has found that William Bradley of
Coventry, gentleman, was himself indicted in Trinity
Term, 1596, for perjury as witness in a Star Chamber
suit.[3] William Bradley was also defendant in Chancery to

1. C 3/217/91; C 2 Eliz. E 1/43. Bradley witnessed the will of Robert
Turnor (Prerogative Court of Canterbury, 78 Sainberbe).
2. K. B. 29/224, m. 110 dorso.
3. K. B. 27/1339, Crown 26 dorso.

Brian Jennings, a baker of Gloucestershire, but this was in 1602.[1] In 1591 Anthony and William Bradley of Lincolnshire were sued by the Queen on a *quo warranto* concerning liberties and franchises in Saxby.[2] There was a family of Bradleys in Cheshire, of whom William of Poynton, yeoman, in 1569 complained in the Star Chamber of riot, and sued in the court of Requests two years earlier; and another William Bradley in Suffolk, whom Margaret Goldinge sued as co-defendant with Edward Rookwood, esquire, concerning copyhold of the latter's manor of Lawshall.[3]

To find the opponent of Marlowe and Watson, however, we must focus our attention upon London. There is no mention of Bradley in the registers of St. Giles, Cripplegate, where he met his death. Yet he must have been buried somewhere, presumably in the parish where he lived, and the problem that faced me was to discover the record of his burial. Such a record would solve the puzzle of the conflicting dates given by the Chancery documents and by the Newgate list for Bradley's death. In which of the hundred and more parishes in and about London was I to look for this essential entry? Here again, court proceedings came to my aid by supplying the necessary clue.

Searching the printed calendar of proceedings in the court of Requests, I found that suit was brought in 1579 by Alice Gravett of High Holborn, widow, and William Barnard of Barnard's Inn, gentleman, against William Bradley of London, marbler.[4] They complained that

1. C 2 Eliz. J 5/10.
2. K. B. 29/227, m. 113 dorso; K. B. 29/230, m. 39; K. B. 27/1320, m. 28.
3. St. Ch. 5, B 3/23; Requests 2/179/60; C 2 Eliz. G 7/34.
4. Requests 2/130/60.

Bradley had not kept his promises made when leasing pasture near Gray's Inn Rails. The same William Bradley, Mr. Hotson was kind enough to inform me, was sued for a debt of sixteen pounds in Michaelmas term, 1583, as William Bradley, citizen and marbler, by John Elkington of Northamptonshire.[1]

Mr. Hotson, however, suggested the identification of Marlowe's adversary with a "Willyam Bradley gent" whom he found listed in arrears for a subsidy payment of 8s. 4d. in the ward of Aldersgate. The name appears only in an affidavit of persons "dead, decayed, or gone out of the said Ward," so that their payments proved uncollectable.[2] The date of this document is the third year of James I (1605–1606). The interval between 1589 and 1605 is a long one, though tax-collectors often carry on a name for some years, still nursing the unconquerable hope.

It seemed to me worth trying to find out more about the Bradley who had dealings in property near Gray's Inn. Accordingly I went to the natural place to look for further information, the parish registers of St. Andrew's, Holborn. There I found at once the name I was seeking:

> William the sonne of William
> Bradley buried the same Daie.

"The same Daie" was September 19, 1589. The entry conclusively established that the record of Gaol Delivery and Watson's pardon were in error when they gave September 28 as the date of the fighting and September 29 for the inquest. Marlowe and Watson evidently fought Bradley on September 18, when they were led to Newgate.

1. K. B. 27/1287, m. 364.
2. E 143/43.

Next day the coroner's jury viewed the body, and Bradley was buried at St. Andrew's.

Having discovered when Bradley was buried, I looked immediately for the entry of his christening. The registers of St. Andrew's are extant only from the beginning of Queen Elizabeth's reign in 1558, but if Bradley was a young man of about Marlowe's age, as I expected to find, he should be there. Among the entries for 1562 I came upon him:

> William Bradley sone of william Bradley was
> Christined the xxviij of october.

His mother's name was probably Ellen as appears from an entry in January, 1564/5:

> Joyse Bradlay daughter of William Bradley & Elline
> his wife was Christinned yᵉ xxviij day.

Another sister, "Elsabethe daughter of William Bradley," was baptized on February 20, 1568/9. An earlier Elizabeth Bradley was married to William Watson on September 4, 1562.

Now that we know the name of Bradley's father also to have been William, we can distinguish between the two in certain other records that mention a William Bradley in Holborn. It is evidently the father who appears in an earlier file of the Middlesex Sessions Rolls.[1] On the night of December 4, 1575, William Bradley was disturbed by a band of sixteen men, armed with swords and daggers, who broke into his house at High Holborn, putting him and all his family in great bodily fear. The rioters beat and wounded Thomas Tayler, clerk, then staying in the house, so that his life was despaired of. The ringleader

---

1. Jeaffreson, *Middlesex County Records*, I, 90.

of the assault was a gentleman of Lyon's Inn, John
Wrighte, abetted by a scrivener and by yeomen from St.
John Street and St. Giles in the Fields. The record yields
the information that when Marlowe's opponent was a
boy of thirteen his father had a house in High Holborn.

Bradley's house was, in fact, an inn, one of the many
conveniently placed in High Holborn to receive the
traveler who rode into London from Oxford or the west.
The father's occupation is established by another interesting record of the Middlesex Sessions.[1] On July 22,
1582, Robert Harrys, Master in Chancery, took the recognizances of Thomas Harrys, "extra barras novi templi
London Jerkynmaker," for his servant Zachary Sherme,
and of Zachary himself, "for woundinge Richard and
w^m the sonnes of w^m Bradley of Greys Inne lane inholder."
The jerkin-maker and his pugnacious prentice made their
appearance in court, and the case was carried over. The
amount of bail for each, twenty pounds, shows that the
skirmish had rather more serious consequences than most
of the kind. Probably other prentices beside Zachary
engaged in the affair, since the two Bradleys got the
worst of it. William was nineteen at the time, Richard
probably at least four years older, inasmuch as his christening does not appear in the registers of St. Andrew,
Holborn, from their beginning in 1558.

The next time a Bradley came before Justice Harrys,
it was not with wounds but with threats to inflict them.
On May 29, 1586, two sureties bound themselves in five
pounds each "pro [Richo] Willo Bradley de Greys Inn
lane pred*icta* Inholder," and William Bradley himself
gave bond in ten pounds that he would keep the peace

1. Sessions Roll 238/13.

toward Thomas Oliver and John Norton.[1] The sureties
were both neighbors, described as of Gray's Inn Lane,
Hugh Bonas, carter, and Gryffin Owen, tailor. Bonas was
the constable of High Holborn. Bradley appeared in court
and was discharged, evidently having dropped his quarrel
with Oliver and Norton. Richard Bradley, whose name
the clerk first set down, probably also had a share in the
quarrel.

In Hilary term of the same year, 28 Elizabeth (1585–
1586), William Bradley of St. Andrew's in Holborn, yeoman, was sued on behalf of the Crown for not repairing
and paving a certain part of the Queen's highway in the
parish, three rods in length, as he was bound to do by his
tenure of lands adjoining. The sheriffs reported in the
same year that Bradley had done the repairing and paving
well and sufficiently.[2] The Queen's highway regularly
refers to High Holborn. Since the Middlesex Sessions
records give High Holborn as Bradley's residence in 1575,
and Gray's Inn Lane in 1582 and 1586, it is probable that
his inn stood at the corner of the two streets, with en-
trances from both. The first of the above records was
found by Mr. Hotson, who has kept a sharp lookout for
William Bradley in his search through the rolls of Queen's
Bench, and has brought to light also the following quarrel.

In Hilary term, 31 Elizabeth, which began in January
before the affray in Hog Lane, Robert Wood brought an
action against William Bradley for assaulting him at Ux-
bridge on September 27, 1588, and wounding and maltreating him so that his life was despaired of. For his
injuries he claimed damages in forty pounds. In defense

1. Sessions Roll 263/25.
2. K. B. 27/1296, before the Crown roll; K. B. 29/222, m. 57.

Bradley replied that on September 27, at High Holborn, Wood spoke to him divers contumelious words, "videlicet inter alias quod idem Willelmus fuit nebulo"—a word which Latin lexicons define as "An idle rascal, a paltry fellow, a scoundrel, a lying rascal, An unthrifty, or vain prodigal, A mere outside, a shadow of a man, a hector, a cowardly bully." No wonder that such a word was more than William could bear. Stirred to just wrath, he grasped his staff and "baculum quasiauit anglice did shake ad prdictum Robertum," saying, "And if it were not for shame I would laye this staffe uppon thy heade." As he held up the staff in this threatening gesture, Robert thrust it at him, whereupon William to protect his body "erexit baculum." These, he assures the court, are all the assaults complained of!

This quick-tempered quarreler in the street might well seem a likely opposite to cross the path of Marlowe and carry the fight to a second adversary, Watson; but we ought to observe that his weapon in Holborn was not cold, gentlemanly steel but the more plebeian quarterstaff. A further record found by Mr. Hotson gives evidence that he was indeed not the William Bradley slain in 1589: for in Hilary, 33 Elizabeth, 1590/91, Wood appeared in court to prosecute the case, and trial was set for the following Easter term.[1] It would be lost labor to prosecute a dead man; and the shake-staff "shadow of a man" may either have been Bradley the elder or a kinsman of John Bradley of "Woxbridge," yeoman, who on December 15, 1586, was killed by the blow of a cowlstaff on the back of his head.[2] The jury found that Robert Ingleton of Ux-

1. K. B. 27/1316, m. 232 dorso.
2. Sessions Roll 266/49.

bridge had murdered Bradley of malice prepense, abetted and comforted by William and Richard Atkyns, who escaped hanging by flight, as Ingleton did by dying.

William Bradley, the innkeeper, was rather an old man to succeed in defending himself so vigorously. In the very year of the assault, on June 16, 1588, I find him as a witness in Chancery, giving his age as sixty-two.[1] He signs by mark: an amusing "B," sitting on top of a "W" which looks more like a "K." He is testifying in the case of Humphrey Harding and his wife *versus* Margaret Sanders, widow, and Richard Bostocke. Margaret was the widow of Nicholas Saunder of Ewell, esquire, whose prodigal heir Nicholas was fleeced by Justice Gardiner.[2] If Mr. Hotson had discussed the Saunder documents, he would no doubt have mentioned that young Nicholas was the dedicatee in 1592 of *Greene's Vision*. As with Shakespeare's *Sonnets*, it was a publisher's dedication: "To the right worshipfull and his especiall good friend, M. Nicholas Sanders of Ewell Esquier, T. Newman wisheth all felicitie." In the same year in which Saunder was selling Gardiner a manor and park for two thousand pounds, Newman described him as "an especiall *Mecenas*, and supporter of learning in these her despised latter daies," and declared, "None haue more insight then you into matters of wit."[3]

An earlier husband of Margaret Saunder, Jasper Fisher, had left her the rents of various houses in Holborn and Gray's Inn Lane. "William Bradley of Grais In Lane aforesaid Inkep*er* of the age of lxij yeres" deposes that he

---

1. C 24/201.

2. Hotson, *Shakespeare versus Shallow* (1931), pp. 73, 238 f., 255 f., 262 f., 285–287, 296, 300, 304–320, 353 f., 359, 361.

3. On Saunder as a friend of Thomas Hariot and Sir Robert Cotton, see Joseph Hunter, *Archæologia*, XXXII (1847), 146.

well knew Master Fisher, who was one of the Six Clerks of the Chancery.[1] Shortly after Fisher died, Bradley took a new lease of ten years from the widow, at a fine of sixteen pounds. From then until Our Lady Day in Lent last past, he has paid his twelve pounds a year rent to Mistress Saunder, "for the howse or In called by the sygne of the Bishoppe at Grais In lanes end." His explicit testimony confirms our inference above that the inn stood at the corner of Gray's Inn Lane and Holborn, just opposite Staple Inn.

The Bishop was one of the oldest inns in Holborn, and for generations the monks of the Charterhouse had held it of the manor of Pancras. The Charterhouse rentals fix its position beyond question. In 1430 the monks were receiving a yearly quit-rent of nine shillings from "Thomas Nanseglos for a tenement called le Bychope at the corner of Portpole." In 1478 the son of William Nanseglos paid for the tenement "above the corner," called "le Busshop." At the dissolution of the monasteries the "quiet rentes" of the Charterhouse still included nine shillings a year from "The Bysshope in Holborne," which now passed into the hands of King Henry VIII.[2]

Bradley lived, then, in Holborn just at the gate of Gray's Inn — a corner which the most famous authors of the next two centuries were to know well. One of the constables of High Holborn in 1664 was a certain Jacob Tonson; and his son Richard published Dryden's *Spanish Friar* and Otway's *Don Carlos* "at *Grays-inn-gate*, in Grays-inn-lane." The shop stood next door to the corner

1. Jasper Fisher was the builder of Fisher's Folly without Bishopsgate (Stow, *A Survey of London* [1908], I, 165 f.; II, 298 f.).
2. Elijah Williams, *Early Holborn and the Legal Quarter of London* (1927), II, nos. 1668–1673.

house, with a back way into what still bore the name, from Bradley's inn, of Bishop's Head Court.[1] Here Richard's brother, the famous Jacob Tonson, published the last poems of Dryden (the *Fables*, 1700) and the earliest of Pope (1709). Above all, "The Works of Mr. *William Shakespear*; in Six Vols. Adorn'd with Cuts," and edited by Nicholas Rowe, was "Printed for *Jacob Tonson*, within *Grays-Inn* Gate, next *Grays Inn* Lane." Steele dined here in 1708 and 1709 and excused himself with notes to "Dear Prue" dated from "Grey's Inn."[2] *The Tatler* for October 12–14, 1710 (no. 237), advertised that "The Shop now in the Possession of Jacob Tonson at Gray's-Inn-Gate is to be let," and Tonson removed to "Shakespear's Head" in the Strand. The shop came later to Thomas Osborne, "the most celebrated bookseller of his day"[3] (confused in the *D. N. B.* with John Osborn, who with Rivington kept urging Samuel Richardson to give them a little book of familiar letters, "and hence," writes Richardson, "sprung Pamela").[4] Here Johnson worked for Osborne on the original *Harleian Miscellany* and on the catalogue of the great Harleian Library, which was sold here. But it was not here that he beat the impertinent bookseller, though legend improved the tale till it made him knock Osborne down with a folio in his own shop.[5]

The innkeeper of the Bishop was evidently a man of consideration among his neighbors. On December 5, 1590, Thomas Cowper, William Bradley, William Roper, and Anthony Wright secured a patent from the Queen granting

---

1. *Early Holborn*, II, no. 1247. See the map at no. 1232.
2. G. A. Aitken, *Life of Steele* (1889) I, 204, 235.
3. T. F. Dibdin, *Bibliomania* (1811), p. 470.
4. *Correspondence*, ed. A. L. Barbauld (1804), I, lxxiii.
5. *Johnsonian Miscellanies* (1897), ed. G. B. Hill, I, 304.

them a sixty years' lease of certain property "to the use of the whole libertie of the highway called High Holborn." Thomas Cowper may have been the juror of that name who the year before had shared in the verdict on Bradley's son. The liberty whose inhabitants thus chose Bradley as one of their trustees consisted of that part of Holborn which the Crown had taken over from the Charterhouse and the hospitals of St. Giles in the Fields and St. John of Jerusalem. The property for which Bradley was a feoffee is described as waste land without Holborn Bars between the highway on the north and on the south a footway leading from Staple Inn to Chancery Lane by a brick wall of the Earl of Southampton's garden. The dwellers in the liberty built upon it their Quest House, which a survey of Parliament describes as containing the room used in 1650 as the schoolhouse, and above stairs a large and spacious Quest Room.[1] The Quest House stood almost exactly over the way from Bradley's inn.

The William Bradley, citizen and marbler, with whom we began our search, can now be identified as the elder Bradley, host of the Bishop "at Grais In lanes ende." An innkeeper often began as apprentice to some other craft, and evidently Bradley had originally belonged to the company of masons and marblers. Only one William Bradley appears in the subsidy lists for High Holborn, assessed at eight pounds in goods in 1586 and on October 27, 1589.[2] In the court of Requests suit mentioned above,[3] Alice Gravett states that she leased to "Willm Bradley of London marbler" one Close of pasture neere Graisine Railes." Bradley promised to allow her every year "a Cowes

---

1. *Early Holborn*, II, nos. 1247, 1248.
2. Harleian MS. 366, f. 85ᵛ; E 179/269/41.   3. Requests 2/130/60.

grasse," which promise "he vtterlie neglected, besides other most vntoward dealing*es*," such as putting her to charges with the parson's tithes and mending the gates, locks, and fences, "w*th* diu*ers* other ill vsages." William Barnard, her brother-in-law, complains that Bradley procured a bond of him "by sinister meanes," and arrested him for the non-payment of thirteen shillings. "Bradley beinge a very troblesome p*er*sone seeketh extreemelie" in the court of Common Pleas to recover the whole penalty of the bond. Bradley's actions were perfectly legal, but they show a forward and grasping mind.

An entry which I have come across in the Controlment Roll for 1591 confirms the identity of William Bradley, marbler. Here he gives bail together with the Hugh Bonas who in 1586 went bail in a similar case for William Bradley of the Bishop. On May 12, 1591, before Sir John Allott, Lord Mayor of London, John Bradley found surety "p*er* Will*elmu*m Bradley Ciuem & mason & marbler london & Hugonem Bonus" of St. Andrew's, Holborn, cutler, that he would keep the peace toward Richard Anderton, clothier. Anderton had personally appeared the same day before the Lord Mayor and taken oath to the following effect: "metuit se de vita sua & mutulac*i*one membror*um* suor*um* sibi fiend*a*" by John Bradley, Thomas Haywarde, and Roger Pynar, yeomen. The Lord Mayor issued a warrant for their arrest. Bradley was released from the Counter in Wood Street on bringing forward William Bradley and Hugh Bonus to give bail that he would keep the peace and appear at the next Gaol Delivery. The other two remained in prison, Haywarde on a bill of trespass and damages in two hundred pounds brought by Anderton in the Mayor's Court at Guildhall and on another claim of damages

brought next day by William Bunday, fletcher.[1] I notice
in the registers of St. Andrew's, Holborn, that a Thomas
Heyward was christened there on October 19, 1565. Ordinarily we should have no record of the foregoing arrests,
but they are recited in the Queen's Bench Controlment
Roll because the prisoners secured a habeas corpus to
bring them before Justice Clenche, at his chamber in
Serjeants' Inn. The Lord Mayor, therefore, had to furnish
an account of the causes of their arrest and imprisonment.
A John Bradley, "servaunt to [M^r] Edwarde Allin," the
actor, was buried at St. Leonard's, Shoreditch, on October
15, 1603, from "Morefield gardons."[2]   But the John arrested in 1591 was more probably William Bradley's son
John, who lived to prove the will of his brother Richard
Bradley of St. Andrew's, Holborn, in 1622.[3]

A William Bradley, who may or may not have been
Bradley of the Bishop Inn, appears time and again as a
juror at Middlesex Sessions. In April, 1580, for example,
when John Brayne and James Burbage were presented
for maintaining unlawful assemblies to hear plays at the
Theater, Bradley was on the list from which the panel
was chosen. He was not pricked to serve till the next
Sessions, but thereafter his name occurs in most of the
following years to May 14, 1589, and again on October 9,
1590. In the next decade I have found his name only in
three panels of the year 1597.[4]   Middlesex jurors were
chosen from a limited list of freeholders, whose names
regularly recur. Since Bradley served in 1590, he cannot

1. K. B. 29/227, m. 100 dorso.

2. Collier in Bodleian MS. Eng. hist. e. 1, f. 30; verified from the register.

3. Archdeaconry of London, Act Book 5, f. 157.

4. Sessions Rolls 225/10, 226/7, 236/5, 238/44, 246/4, 248/57, 252/32,
275/6, 283/39, 295/19, 346/20, 349/11, 350/53, 411/45.

have been the younger William, but he may have been William the father.

The man with whom Marlowe fought, then, was a young Londoner twenty-six years of age, Marlowe himself at the time being only twenty-five. Already seven years earlier Bradley had been in a fray with a jerkin-maker's prentice, who wounded him and his brother Richard. Little else is known of him until the day he met Marlowe and Watson in Hog Lane. He was not a student at the Inns of Court, for the first William to appear in the admission registers of any of the four Inns is a William Bradley, gentleman, who entered Gray's Inn from Barnard's Inn on February 11, 1593/4.[1] An earlier William Bradley matriculated from St. John's, Cambridge, the college of Greene and Nashe, in the Easter term of 1580.[2] At that time Bradley of Holborn was seventeen, the same age at which Marlowe came up to the university in the year following. The St. John's man, however, matriculated as a pensioner, and this status, though not impossible, would have been unusual for the son of an innkeeper.

There is one record, however, which unquestionably refers to the right William Bradley. In the Queen's Bench Controlment Rolls, of which he was the first to make a thorough examination, Mr. Hotson discovered the following entry, which he has most generously given me to publish:

Anglia ss   Will*elmu*s Bradley pet*it* secur*itates* pac*is* v*er*sus Hug*on*em Swyft & Joh*ann*em Allen & Thomam Watson ob met*um* mortis &c

Atta*chiamentum* vic*ecomiti* Midd*lesex* re*tornabile* xv*e* m*artini

---

1. Joseph Foster, *The Register of Admissions to Gray's Inn* (1889), p. 83.
2. J. Venn and J. A. Venn, *Alumni Cantabrigienses*, I (1922), 201.

The date is 1589, for it occurs among the entries for Michaelmas term, 31–32 Elizabeth.[1]

This record is precisely similar to the one in which William Wayte, seven years later, asked for sureties of the peace against William Shakespere, Francis Langley, Dorothy, wife of John Soer, and Anne Lee.[2] Bradley is petitioning a justice of the Queen's Bench to have Watson and two companions enter bond, in Elizabethan language, "to the good abearing": that is, to find two sufficient sureties to join with each in giving bond to keep the peace towards the petitioner. What makes the record especially significant is its date. The fifteenth of St. Martin, when the sheriff was directed to cause Bradley's adversaries to appear at Westminster Hall, fell on November 25. The attachment was destined never to be executed, for when that day came Bradley had long been safe from all threatening, in the grave.

Bradley's petition, it is important to notice, was entered on the Controlment Rolls under Michaelmas term. Yet Bradley was killed in September, while Michaelmas term did not begin until October 9. It becomes sufficiently evident, then, that to seek protection against one's enemies it was not necessary to wait until term opened. Bradley's coming before a justice may have occurred at any time after the close of Trinity term, which in 1589 ended on June 18. The clerk would then close the records for the past term and begin afresh with entries that looked forward toward the term to come, in this case Michaelmas term. The evidence of the Controlment Roll, therefore, dates the quarrel, not in the autumn, but at some time in the summer of 1589.

1. K. B. 29/226.   2. Hotson, *Shakespeare versus Shallow*, p. 9.

Bradley had invoked the law in vain, and the event proved that his petition was not one of those made out of mere malice, but that he had only too good cause for his fear of death or bodily harm. The importance of the entry in the Controlment Rolls is that it furnishes clear proof that the fray in which Watson came to Marlowe's assistance was not a sudden or casual brawl in the streets, but a meeting between men who were already at odds. "Art thou now come?" said Bradley as he caught sight of Watson rushing in; and his words can be seen to imply that the new opponent was one whom he had been expecting. Marlowe was fighting in his friend's quarrel, and when Watson came up one may reasonably doubt whether it was to play the part of peacemaker, as the coroner's jury found, or to take on his share of a combat that was properly his own.

Marlowe and Watson were indeed arrested, as the Newgate docket tells us, on suspicion of murder. Such a charge was probably made as a matter of common practise after any violent death, but in this case there was especially good ground for putting it forward at the start, subject to further investigation. Watson might well be suspected of malice aforethought by any officer who had knowledge of his feud with the slain man. By the time he was lodged in Newgate the authorities would presumably have made sufficient inquiries to learn that Bradley had recently sworn before a justice of the Queen's Bench that Watson was seeking his bodily injury or death. It was fortunate for Watson that the coroner's jury decided, on the testimony, let us hope, of impartial witnesses, that he had intervened only to stop Bradley's fight with Marlowe, and that he had done his best not to wound his opponent until he was pressed literally to the last ditch.

Thomas Watson is a common name; but if any doubt remained that Marlowe's ally was the poet of *A Passionate Century of Love*, the name of Hugh Swift among Bradley's adversaries on the Controlment Roll would be enough to set it at rest. For Thomas Watson married, at St. Antholin's on September 6, 1585, Anne Swift; [1] and her brother Thomas, whom Watson assisted in a scheme to claim in marriage his master's daughter Frances Cornwallis, testified when examined in Star Chamber in 1593/4 that he had procured his brother Hugh Swift to write the bill which he got Frances to sign under the impression that it was a promise to pay, whereas it was a contract to marry. It was Hugh who had advised him that the word "irrecoverable was the naturall and binding woord." [2]

From the fact that Bradley sought the protection of the law it does not necessarily follow that Watson and his friends had begun the quarrel. Francis Langley, we remember, had himself petitioned sureties of the peace against Wayte some time before Wayte sought them against Shakespeare and Langley. In looking up Mr. Hotson's reference to the Controlment Rolls, therefore, I kept my eyes open for petitions by any of the three men — Swift, Allen, and Watson — whom Bradley named as threatening his death. I was rewarded by finding the following record:

1. *Harleian Society Registers*, VIII (1883), 31.

2. Star Chamber 5, C 33/38. I have found the pleadings in the Crown prosecution, Attorney General v. Swift, Star Chamber 7, 1/6, and Coke's examination of Thomas Swift, Star Chamber 5, A 36/5. See also J. S. Burn, *The Star Chamber* (1870), p. 71; and the many papers on the case in Bodleian Tanner MSS. 97, 283, 285, 286.

Angl*ia* ss   Hugo Swyfte pet*it* secur*itates* pacis v*er*sus Georgiu*m*
             Orrell ob met*um* mortis &c
                         Att*achiamentum* vic*ecomiti* Midd*lesex* re-
                         tornabile xv*e* m*artini*

The entry occurs on the same membrane that records the
petition of Bradley, but on the recto instead of the dorso.
From their relative positions we infer that Swift was one
lap ahead of Bradley in resorting to the law. Bradley was
not far behind, since both sides were ordered to furnish
sureties on the same day, the fifteenth of Martinmas.

Swift's petition takes us one step farther back into the
origin of the enmity that led to Bradley's death. If it
proves possible to find out anything more about the
causes of that enmity, it will probably be through tracing
out the respective histories of Swift and of Orrell. For
I find in the registers of St. Andrew, Holborn, that "George
Orrell was Christined the xj day of marche," 1564/5. He
was therefore a younger neighbor of Bradley, and as
such a natural ally against the party of Swift, Allen, and
Watson. He must, indeed, have lived just over the way
from Bradley, for he is described as dwelling in the "end of
Grays Inn Lane." Records prove that the eastern corner
of Gray's Inn Lane and Holborn was occupied by George's
father, Peter Orrell, victualer, who had other sons christened at St. Andrew's, as did Thomas Orrell, cook, also of
Gray's Inn Lane.[1] Peter Orrell was indicted in Queen's
Bench in 1586 for encroaching on the highway in Holborn
south of his house with divers posts and bars, and on
Gray's Inn Lane west of his house with a wooden erection
for shops, so that people could not pass by, until the Crown

1. Will of John Orrell, Prerogative Court of Canterbury, 94 Cobham.

forced their removal.[1] In another Coram Rege Roll his
name is found on the dorso of a membrane that mentions
Shakespeare, for the same attorney, John Harborne, acted
for Shakespeare's father in suing John Lambert and for
George Ognell, the rich mercer who bought Stoneleigh
Court in Warwickshire, in recovering a debt of 160 *l.* from
Peter Orrell of High Holborn, yeoman.[2]

A Middlesex jury indicted George Orrell of Holborn and
Allan Starlinge of Holborn, yeomen, for breaking into the
dwelling house of Aaron Holland at High Holborn on April
6, 1592, assaulting Holland and his wife Elizabeth, and
maltreating them in such fashion that their lives were despaired of.[3] Aaron Holland is known in theatrical history
as the builder and owner of the Red Bull playhouse in St.
John Street. His residence is given as Gray's Inn Lane in
the subsidy roll of October, 1589.[4] I have found at St.
Andrew's the record of his marriage to Elizabeth Tomson
on August 20, 1581. His appearances in Middlesex Sessions Rolls and other records are unusually frequent.

A vivid description of George Orrell's actions on the day
of Essex's rebellion is preserved at Hatfield.[5] William Rey-
nolds wrote Cecil that he was surprised to see omitted from
the list of Essex's confederates

the names of two men which I saw in the troop which charged
my Lord Burghley your brother and the king of heralds in Gra-
cious Street. One of them is called Captain or Lieutenant Orrell,
a follower of the lord Montegle, a most desperate rakehell as

1. K. B. 9/664, no. 4; K. B. 29/222, m. 50 dorso; K. B. 29/229, m. 53. See
also Middlesex Sessions Roll 236/3; Harleian MS. 366, f. 86; E 179/269/41.
2. K. B. 27/1311, m. 516 dorso and Crown 97.
3. Sessions Roll 308/96.
4. E 179/269/41.
5. Historical MSS. Commission, *Calendar of the MSS. . . . at Hatfield House,*
XI (1906), 46; cf. p. 44, and XIV (1923), 171.

lives. He dwells in end of Grays Inn Lane, a freeholder of 40 *l.*
the year, as some say. . . . Orrell before mentioned, who holds
his neck awry, did run and leap in the forefront with Sir Christopher Blunt and Mr. Busshell, their weapons drawn, crying
"Saw, Saw, Saw, Saw, tray, tray."

Captain George Orrell was also named as a conspirator
in the confession of Sir John Davies, and he was accordingly imprisoned in Wood Street Counter. The day after
Southampton was condemned to death, nine of the rebels
were led to the bar; but just as they were holding up their
hands to take the oath, a letter came from the Queen,
declaring that she was informed by Fulk Greville that
many had been drawn into rebellion unwittingly, and
therefore ordering that only three more should undergo
judgment: Sir Edmund Baynham, John Littleton, and
George "Orwell." Baynham and Orrell pleaded ignorance
and said that they followed the Earls "*ex observantia*," but
together with Littleton they were condemned to death.
John Chamberlain wrote on February 24 that Essex was
to lead the way, but that these three were expected to
follow "thicke and threfold." [1]

Baynham saved his life by a cash payment to Sir Walter
Raleigh for a pardon, and conveyed his manor of Pow-
ershall or Little Witham in Essex to Raleigh's trustees,
Nicholas Fortescue and John Shelbery. [2] When Littleton
died in King's Bench prison in July, 1601, Baynham was
still in prison, but Orrell was "abroad." [3] Camden in his
manuscript of the *Annales* [4] describes Orrell as "veteranus

---

1. *Letters Written by John Chamberlain during the Reign of Elizabeth*, Camden
Society (1861), p. 106; S. P. Dom. Eliz. 278/46, 103, 110; William Camden,
Annales Rerum Anglicarum et Hibernicarum Regnante Elizabetha (Leyden, 1625),
p. 801.　　　　　　　　　　　　　2. Close Roll, 42 Eliz.: C 54/1693.
3. S. P. Dom. Eliz. 281/67.　　　4. Ed. 1717, III, 858.

incurvicervicus," "the old soldier with a wry neck," though the published editions omit the last word and sometimes both. The old soldier went back to the life that suited him best, for in October, 1601, he was awaiting a command in Ireland as "Captain Orrell, a tall man, a follower of Lord Mounteagle." [1] He served in the Earl of Thomond's camp when Lord Mountjoy besieged the Spaniards in Kinsale, and after the town was taken Sir George Carew asked Secretary Cecil to find him further employment. Carew wrote that he had witnessed Orrell's "vallor and good carriadg during the siedge," and "that he refused no service were yt never soe full of danger." [2] James I in 1607 granted George Orrell [3] the property forfeited by his attainder for high treason, consisting of the house his father, Peter Orrell, had occupied, and three more "in Houlborne alias Grayes Inn lane alias Purpole lane."

Orrell, then, valiant soldier or "a most desperate rakehell as lives," was in 1589 threatening to kill or injure Hugh Swift, Watson's brother-in-law. Probably Orrell entered into the affair on behalf of his friend, for Bradley's death, so far as is known, put an end to the fighting. Swift survived, for he took part in the Cornwallis affair, and Mr. Hotson has found him acting as an attorney in Queen's Bench in 1595.[4] Since he was an attorney, he must have belonged to one of the Inns of Chancery, perhaps to one of the several situated in Holborn, not far from the homes of

---

1. *Calendar of the State Papers Relating to Ireland, 1601–3* (1912), p. 113.
2. *Calendar*, p. 290 (the original letter names only "Cap^n Orrell"; there was also a Captain Lewis Orrell in Ireland, but throughout 1601 he was stationed in Donegal, so that the editor's identification with George Orrell is correct).
3. Patent Roll, 5 James I: C 66/1746.
4. K. B. 27/1335, m. 588.

both Bradley and Orrell at the corner of Gray's Inn Lane, facing Staple Inn.

The other associate of Watson against whom Bradley swore the peace, John Allen, was probably the brother of Edward Alleyn, the renowned actor of Tamburlaine, Barabas, and Dr. Faustus. Earlier in 1589, John Alleyn was a sharer with Edward in "playinge apparelles, playe Bookes, Instrumentes and other commodities." He was in London during the summer in question, for in August he bought for five pounds a long cloak of black velvet, lined with taffeta, and in July the Privy Council wrote Alderman Harte and others to take order on his behalf in a dispute with Dr. Thomas Martyn, the civilian.[1] Like Marlowe and Watson, he lived not far from the Theater, for he is described in 1587/8 as "John Allen, of St. Botolph's without Bishopsgate, innholder." He and his brother Edward in 1585 bought of their mother and step-father four messuages in Bishopsgate Street adjoining Fisher's Folly[2] — then occupied by the Earl of Oxford and soon afterward by William Cornwallis, when he employed Watson there as tutor to his son. The Alleyns inherited from their father other property in St. Botolph's; but John described himself in May, 1592, as late of that parish,[3] and at his death, before May 4, 1596, his residence is given as St. Andrew's, Holborn. His widow Margaret, however, on July 2, was of St. Botolph's, where her

1. W. W. Greg, *Henslowe Papers* (1907), pp. 31–32; G. F. Warner, *Catalogue of the Manuscripts and Muniments of Alleyn's College of God's Gift at Dulwich* (1881), pp. 3, 85–86; J. P. Collier, *The Alleyn Papers* (Shakespeare Society, 1843), pp. 5–6. I notice that among the signatures to the Council's letter, in place of the Earl of Warwick, Collier unobtrusively inserts "Edward Dyer."

2. Warner, *Catalogue*, pp. 251, 252.

3. C. W. Wallace, *The First London Theatre*, University of Nebraska Studies, XIII (1913), 124.

husband had leased two houses from her mother, widow
Julian Cropwell.[1] There is no warrant for the statement
(by Greg, Nungezer, and the indexer of Warner's *Catalogue*) that John Alleyn owned the Unicorn or other
property in St. Saviour's; for it was in 1618 that this
property was "late in the tenure" (by lease, not owner-
ship) of a John Allen,[2] whether the younger John or
another of the name. I have found a number of lawsuits
concerning John Alleyn, including a Chancery deposition
on his behalf made on May 28, 1593, by Edward Alleyn of
St. Saviour's, gentleman, aged twenty-seven.[3]

So many John Allens were living near Watson in 1589
that only a few of the others beside the actor can be mentioned. John Allen of Clerkenwell, yeoman, servant to the
right honorable Earl of Derby, testified in Chancery that
in 1585 he had witnessed a deed to his then master, Ralph
Bott, in Mr. Delahaye's house in the Spital without Bishopsgate.[4] He was forty-five years old, and signed by a
mark. The Middlesex Sessions Rolls mention a John Allen
of Clerkenwell who kept an unlawful alehouse in 1579;
one whose house in Turnmill Street was broken into in
1591; John Allen of Norton Folgate, shoemaker, surety in

---

1. Warner, *Catalogue*, pp. 125, 127, 255–256 (where, misunderstanding memo-
randa by Edward Alleyn, Warner wrongly takes the lease to be of the Boar's
Head on the Bankside). The convenient biography of John Alleyn given by
Edwin Nungezer, *A Dictionary of Actors* (New Haven, 1929), pp. 11–12, overlooks Greg, *Henslowe's Diary*, I (1904), 6, and II (1908), 239, T. W. Baldwin,
The Organization and Personnel of the Shakespearean Company (Princeton, 1927),
Appendix I, and the fact that Alleyn's wife was daughter of Julian Cropwell,
buried at St. Botolph's in February, 1595/6 (who was probably widow of Robert
Cropwell, buried there on January 11, 1579/80: see A. W. C. Hallen, *The Registers of St. Botolph, Bishopsgate, London* (1889), I, 285, 317.
2. Warner, *Catalogue*, p. 269.
3. C 24/233/2.
4. C 24/201, Ralph Bott, defendant, *v.* Edmund More and others, plaintiffs.

1587/8; and a John Allen of Finsbury, yeoman, ordered on February 13, 1594/5, to appear before the justices at Westminster together with James "Burbache" of Holywell Street and others.[1] John Alleyn the actor had dealings in 1593 with a John Allyn of St. Giles without Cripplegate.[2] There was even another actor John Allen, as appears from the following entry for 1597 in the register of St. Botolph's without Bishopsgate:[3]

> Jone uxor Johis Allen playe^r ye 18 octob^r
> bur ye same tyme hir child, still borne.

Joan seems to have had a daughter, thus christened in 1596:

Bennett ye Reput daug' of Jno Allen 26 Julij wch Jno went wth S^r ffr Drak to ye Indians in wch tyme this child was got by a stage playe^r.

There are plenty of other occurrences of the name John Allen at St. Botolph's beside the few cited by Collier and repeated by Chambers and Nungezer.[4] At least four men of the name lived there during the fifteen-nineties, for, beside the brother of Edward and the man whose wife died in 1597, one John was buried on May 18 and another on August 20, 1593. The younger John, Edward's nephew, may have been the John, son of John Allen, christened on August 9, 1584; but another John, son of John, was christened on September 3, 1592. The son of John Allen christened in 1588, whom Collier gives as "Lowin"

1. Sessions Rolls 220/2, 297/25, 276/14, 326/1.
2. Warner, *Catalogue*, p. 124.
3. Collier cites the entry in Bodleian MS. Eng. hist. e. 1, f. 133^v. Hallen, *The Registers of St. Botolph, Bishopsgate, London*, I, 321, omits the word "player." My quotation is from the original register.
4. Chambers, *The Elizabethan Stage*, II, 299; Nungezer, *A Dictionary of Actors*, pp. 2–3.

(suggesting the name of the later actor of Hamlet, then a boy of twelve), appears in the register as "Lewen." [1]

Which of all the John Allens was William Bradley's enemy? If we had no further evidence, it would be impossible to say that one was more likely than another. Fortunately, there is preserved at Dulwich College a bond bearing date March 8, 30 Eliz. (1588).[2] By this document William Bradley of London, yeoman, binds himself in a penalty of forty marks to pay fourteen pounds on August 25 following to John Allen of London, innholder. This bit of parchment makes it almost certain that the John Allen whom Bradley feared was the actor's brother, manager of the Admiral's Men at the Theater. If that is correct, here at last we have succeeded in discovering a clue to the character of Bradley's relations with one of the men against whom he desired protection. He had owed money to Alleyn, and his bond had fallen due a year before he was killed. If he had paid it, the bond would have been canceled and returned to Bradley to be disposed of. Since it is not canceled, he had evidently failed to pay it at the day, and Alleyn accordingly kept it for the purpose of bringing suit upon it in the Common Pleas. Such a suit, or even the threat of it, made an excellent beginning for a personal feud. Hugh Swift's part in the affair may have been that of Alleyn's attorney; and Watson was both Swift's brother-in-law and a writer of plays, probably for the Theater.

1. Hallen, I, 119; parish register.
2. Muniments, no. 94; Warner, *Catalogue*, p. 252.

CHAPTER IV

Marlowe's Sureties

AFTER the killing of Bradley on September 18, 1589, Marlowe for nearly two weeks lay prisoner in Newgate. He was entitled to bail, but who would offer it for him? Poetry could not help him in his predicament. Neither Kyd nor Nashe nor any other of his playwright friends was rich enough to give sufficient surety. The law required bail from two subsidy men, persons of assured income rated in the Queen's books. At last, on October 1, Marlowe found two men of substance willing to give bond for his reappearance at the Gaol Delivery and thus to set him free. These two men deserve to be remembered as Marlowe's friends in need: Richard Kitchen of Clifford's Inn, gentleman, and Humphrey Rowland of East Smithfield, horner.

Sir Sidney Lee and Mr. J. H. Ingram could find out nothing about Marlowe's two sureties. Mr. Tucker Brooke, however, searching the Ancient Indictments at the Record Office, found a very interesting indictment of Richard Kitchen in 1594 for assaulting and wounding John Finch with a dagger. In his article called "Marlowe among the Churchwardens" in *The Atlantic Monthly* for July, 1926, Mr. Hotson told of Mr. Brooke's discovery and described his own efforts to trace the careers of Kitchen and Rowland in the hope of throwing further light on Marlowe. By a diligent search through the rolls of the Queen's Bench he found Kitchen acting as an attorney in 1586, and in the subsidy rolls he found Kitchen assessed in the parish of St. Bartholomew the Great. Beyond these brief records, Richard Kitchen remained only a name.

Something can now be added to our knowledge of the two men who secured Marlowe's release from Newgate. Without making a special search for Richard Kitchen of Clifford's Inn, I have come across him fairly frequently in documents at the Record Office. Even before I found the inquisition on Bradley or any of the other records in this book, I had met Kitchen as a witness in the Attorney General's Star Chamber suit against Sir Edmund Baynham and others, testifying on behalf of his friend William Williamson, host of the Mermaid in Bread Street.[1] Kitchen turns up more than once, also, as a witness in the Town Depositions in Chancery. Perhaps he may be recognized even in so familiar a source as *Henslowe's Diary*, though the strange disguise of Henslowe's spelling has kept the surname from being identified.

In following the trail of Richard Kitchen of Clifford's Inn, we must first of all keep him distinct from the other Richard Kitchens of his time with whom he might be confused. One of the name had been a fellow of Marlowe's college at Cambridge, Corpus Christi, as early as 1548; ejected from his fellowship under Queen Mary, he became in Elizabeth's reign rector of Stisted and Inworth, Essex, and died in 1599. Another Richard Kitchin of Essex matriculated as a pensioner of Christ's College, Cambridge, in 1580, took his B.A. at Queens' in 1587/8, and in 1591 became rector of Hadleigh, Essex.[2] No Richard appears in Clark's *Register of the University of Oxford* or in Foster's

1. Star Chamber 5, A 1/29.
2. J. Venn and J. A. Venn, *Alumni Cantabrigienses*, III (1924), 26.

Alumni Oxonienses; but in a Chancery deposition[1] of October 10, 1588, I find "Ri. kichen of the Cite of oxon. and Scoller of thage of xxxviij yeres." He may be distinguished from Marlowe's friend through his signature, "by me Richarde Kytchin." His testimony that in 1581 he witnessed a deed to John Estmonde of the University of Oxford, Bachelor of Law, is corroborated by "Jo. kichen of the Cite of Oxon and student there," who signs himself "John Kechin." A Richard Kitchin was at Lewisham, Kent, in 1590.[2] Richard Kichen of Albury, Surrey, gentleman, made his will on September 22, 1595, leaving the bulk of his estate to his brothers John and Thomas, who as executors proved the will on October 15 following.[3] In 1604 one of the richer residents of Lincolnshire was a Richard Kitchin, from whom James I required a benevolence of twenty pounds.[4] A later Richard lived at Totteridge, Herts., in 1612, and in 1634 gave his arms to the heralds as son of Robert Kitchin of London and grandson of Robert of Leeds.[5]

The document which makes it possible to place Marlowe's friend Richard Kitchen is his will, a source of information which until now has been overlooked. The will is at Somerset House[6] and is brief enough to be printed in full:

October the nine and twentith

In the name of god Amen I Richarde Kitchin of Cliffor*des* Inne being of p*er*fect memorie doe make my last will and testa-

---

1. C 24/204/27.
2. C 2 Eliz. W 16/40, William Weycoe v. Robert Ashe and others.
3. Prerogative Court of Canterbury, 71 Scott.
4. Cambridge University Library MS. F. f. 2. 28.
5. S. P. Dom. Chas. I 159/58, 165/57, 58; *The Visitations of Herts.*, Harleian Society, XXII (1886), 70.
6. Prerogative Court of Canterbury, 86 Harte.

m^t: in manner and forme following videlicet first I bequeath my soule to almightie god, And my bodie to be buried at the discrecion of my Executor Item I doe giue vnto Annes my wife the house in Skipton and the (blank) closes withall thappurtenaunc*es* thereunto belonginge during her naturall life, And after her decease to the heires males of Abell kitchin of Bristow All other my goodes and chattells moueable and vnmoueable I giue to my wife And doe constitute her my sole Executrix. In Witnesse whereof I haue putt to my hande the daie and yere first aboue written. *per* me Rich*ard*um Kitchin. Sealed and deliuered in presence vs ffrauncis kitchin Allin Craiford Cutbert Crayford.

Kitchen died in 1604, for the will was proved on November 17 of that year by his widow Agnes (written in the will, according to the usual Elizabethan pronunciation, Annes). He had been married since 1579/80, when he secured a general license from the Bishop of London bearing date January 28:[1] "Richard Kitchen, Gent., of Clifford's Inn, & Agnes Redman, Spinster, of St Swithin's, London." William Redman of St. Swithin's made a will only five lines long on January 16, 1586/7, proved on January 26, bequeathing his goods "to my sonne James and my daughter Agnes."[2] Redman was assessed at five pounds in the subsidy roll for Walbrook ward in 1582,[3] which indicates an average income but no particular wealth for Kitchen to inherit. The Francis Kitchin who witnessed Richard's will may have been "Francis Kitchyn, Clerk, Curate of St Michael Bassishaw," licensed in 1581 to marry Eleanor Aston.[4] Francis Kitchen was rector of St. Clement's, East-

---

1. *Allegations for Marriage Licences Issued by the Bishop of London, 1520 to 1610*, Harleian Society, XXV (1887), 94.
2. Prerogative Court of Canterbury, 3 Spencer.
3. E 179/251/16.
4. *Allegations for Marriage Licences*, p. 103.

cheap, from 1590 to 1595, and in 1598 one of the name was curate of Bromley St. Leonard, Middlesex.[1]

Richard Kitchen himself answers the question of his origin by the disposal in his will of "the house in Skipton." For many generations Kitchens had been living at Skipton in Craven, in the West Riding of Yorkshire, some of them in the service of the great baronial family of the Cliffords, lords of Skipton Castle. One of the Cliffords, Matilda of York, widow of Richard, Earl of Cambridge, Edward IV's grandfather, bequeathed five marks to John Kechyn in 1446. Other Kitchens received bequests as members of the household in the wills of John, Lord Scrope, in 1455; of Sir John Pilkington, who died at Skipton in 1478; and of William Copley, a rich lawyer, who in 1490 left "to Richard Kechyne my bootes and spores."[2] The most interesting record of the Kitchens is testimony in a cause before the Council of the North begun in 1540/41, in which the Nortons denied the Cliffords' right to hunt in Rylstone lordship, the scene of Wordsworth's *The White Doe of Rylstone*. The Cliffords had several of their foresters examined to prove that Rylstone was within the forest of Skipton:[3]

Robert Kitchen, of Skipton, of the age of 70 years, deposeth, That he hath been at divers views and ranges of the deer in the forest of Skipton, at the commandment of master Henry Popeley, forster to my lord's father that now is. They began to range at the Round Topt Esh, and from thence to Flasby, and so to Eshton, thence to Rilston, and so to Burnsal.

1. Richard Newcourt, *Repertorium*, I (1708), 327, 920; cf. H. F. Waters, *Genealogical Gleanings in England* (1901), II, 1359.

2. *Testamenta Eboracensia*, II, Surtees Society, XXX (1855), 122, 193; III, Surtees Society, XLV (1865), 239; IV, Surtees Society, LIII (1869), 50.

3. T. D. Whitaker, *The History and Antiquities of the Deanery of Craven, in the County of York* (1878), pp. 305–306.

Robert Kitchin, of Skipton, yeoman, aet. 60, deposeth, That he was one of the Forsters of the Old Park of Skipton twenty-three years; hath hunted and chased out the deer in Rilston Lordship to every other place where he would in the forest of Skipton; he did see my old lady Clifford hunt in Rilston Lordship, and set the hounds and greyhounds, and kill two bucks there, and carry them off; and Thomas Garth, keeper at that time, had the shulders for his fee; and there was with her, at one course, Sir Thomas Tempest, knight, Sir Thomas Darcy, knight, Master Viewers, and many others; and this deponent saith he hath walked there an hundred times as Forester and Keeper of the Old Park.

The Clifford to whom Kitchin was forester was Henry, the Shepherd Lord, he who knew "The silence that is in the starry sky, The sleep that is among the lonely hills." [1] The ballad of *The Rising in the North* [2] keeps green the memory of Norton and his "nine good sonnes"; but the only record of the insurrection of 1569 that remains among the evidences at Bolton Abbey is the listing among the tenantry of "Richard Kitchen, butler to Mr. Norton, who rose in rebellion with his master, and was executed at Ripon." [3] This note is found in a survey of Rylstone made after the attainder in 1570 of old Richard Norton, who had borne the banner of the rebel earls at Branspeth Castle and who died an exile in Flanders in 1588, at the reported age of one hundred. The faithful butler was not the only Kitchen at Rylstone, for wills of many others are in the registry at York, from John, buried at Our Lady of Rylstone in 1541, to Christopher in 1576 and Lionel in 1597. [4] Rylstone is in Airedale only six miles north of Skipton.

1. Wordsworth, *Song at the Feast of Brougham Castle, upon the Restoration of Lord Clifford, the Shepherd, to the Estates and Honours of his Ancestors* (1809).
2. Thomas Percy, *Reliques of Ancient English Poetry* (1891), I, 266.
3. Whitaker, *The History and Antiquities of the Deanery of Craven*, p. 521.
4. *Index of Wills in the York Registry*, Yorkshire Archæological Society,

Marlowe's friend Kitchen, since he left his estate to the heirs of Abel Kitchen, was probably either son or nephew to Gabriel Kitchen of Skipton, yeoman, who named as executors of his will in 1591 his son Gabriel and daughter Elizabeth and as supervisors his sons Christopher and Abel.[1] Gabriel Kitchen bought a house in Skipton as early as 1556,[2] and in 1563, together with his son Thomas, he proved the will of his father Thomas Kitchen of Skipton.[3] The younger Gabriel died in 1603, but his mother Agnes, widow of Gabriel the elder, lived until 1613/14, when she was buried in the church, "aged about 102." [4]

Richard Kitchen of Clifford's Inn, then, came from a family whose members had been foresters to the Lords Clifford and had marched with the "goodly train" that went to war with the Nortons from "Rylstone's old sequestered Hall." [5] Is it a coincidence that Kitchen, coming up to London from Skipton, the chief residence of the Cliffords, should have entered Clifford's Inn rather than any other Inn of Chancery? Perhaps; but it is interesting to notice that when the Earl of Cumberland in 1618 granted the fee of Clifford's Inn to the society, he specifically reserved the use of a chamber there for a member of the inn employed in his affairs, a right which his heirs did not part with until 1880.[6] His father, George Clifford, Earl of Cumberland from 1570 to 1605, probably likewise employed as

Record Series, XI (1891), 101; XIX (1895), 95; XXIV (1898), 62. Cf. *North Country Wills*, II, Surtees Society, CXXI (1912), 210.

1. York Registry, vol. 25, f. 1125.
2. *Feet of Fines of the Tudor Period*, I, Yorkshire Archæological Society, Record Series, II (1887), 194 (cf. James Ketchyn on p. 240).
3. York Registry, vol. 17, f. 230.
4. W. J. Stavert, *The Parish Register of Skipton-in-Craven, 1592–1680* (1894), pp. 36, 51.
5. Wordsworth, *The White Doe of Rylstone*.
6. William Page, *Clifford's Inn* (1921), p. 18.

his attorney one or more members of the inn, for the indenture of 1618 merely reaffirmed the existing covenants. Clifford's Inn was the oldest of the Inns of Chancery, having been granted to Robert de Clifford in 1310 and rented in 1344 to the "apprentices of the Bench." In the hall of the inn, which still stands behind the church of St. Dunstan's in the West, the members dined at two tables: an upper one for the Principal and "Rules," or elder members of the society, and a lower one for the juniors, known as the "Kentish Mess." In 1586 the inn had one hundred and ten members, some attorneys, and some students preparing to enter the Inner Temple, as the most famous members of Clifford's Inn did: Edward Coke in 1572 and John Selden in 1604.[1]

Kitchen belonged to Clifford's Inn from before the time of his marriage in 1580 down to his death in 1604. He made his living, therefore, as an attorney. Mr. Hotson in *The Atlantic Monthly* mentioned a case in the Coram Rege Rolls for Hilary term, 1586, in which Richard Kitching appeared in the court of Queen's Bench as attorney for Thomas Meeres of Kent. Kitchen himself describes another case in Queen's Bench in a Chancery deposition, testifying on behalf of Richard Arnold, defendant to John Stower.[2] "Rychard Keechin of London gen*tleman* of the age of xxxv yeres," on February 8, 1588/9, bore witness that he had often heard Stower call Arnold "brooker/ vsurar/ Extorci*o*ner/ A com*m*en taker of advauntag*es* of bond*es*/ & A cutt throte," and say that he, Stower, "ment to plage him, w^t sondry accons that shuld cost him more money / then the value of the bonde forfettures & all." The bond was made to Anthony Martyn, goldsmith, in whose name

1. Page, *Clifford's Inn*, pp. 19–20.   2. C 24/203/3 (also numbered 38).

Arnold sued his neighbor Stower and secured execution by his attorney Mr. Trussell — Henry Trussell, of the family long seated at Billesley near Stratford-upon-Avon, and father, I believe, of John Trussell the poet. Trussell reported the progress of the execution to Arnold and Kitchen.

Marlowe's imprisonment in Newgate happened later in the same year, when Kitchen and Rowland came to his rescue. Not long afterward Kitchen testified again in a case which involved Dr. Hector Nuñez, the Jewish physician, whose name Marlowe used when in *The Jew of Malta* [1] he made Barabas include among the wealthy Jews "Nones in Portugal." On the last day of January, 1589/90, "Rycharde Keechin of Cliffordes In gentleman of the age of xxxj yeres" deposed on behalf of his client Thomas Holmes, esquire, against Bartholomew Corsino, merchant stranger.[2] Within his study in Clifford's Inn, Kitchen testified, "Ennegro de Balderano Straunger" told him "w^t great lamentacion & repentant Wordes" that he had made a false oath (in the court of Requests) at the persuasion of Alonso de Basurto, solicitor in this cause to Corsino, "and did most hartelly cry god mercy for the same." He swore falsely because Alonso and Dr. Hector promised to give him a piece of money. On hearing his confession Kitchen desired Inigo to go with him to the King's Bench prison, where Basurto was lying for debt, and charged the latter with subornation of perjury, which he denied. "Well," said Kitchen to the prisoner,

1. Ed. H. S. Bennett (1931), p. 44 (I. i. 123). On Dr. Nuñez see Lucien Wolf, "Jews in Elizabethan England," Jewish Historical Society of England, *Transactions*, vol. XI (1928).

2. C 24/194/32. Cf. the wills of George Holmes (1580) and of Thomas Holmes (1591), Prerogative Court of Canterbury, 10 Darcy and 21 Sainberbe.

this geare is nought and it will falle out one daye ill favo^rdly
against yo^u/ But Mr Allonso qd this depo^t, this po^r man sayyth
and protesteth yo^u owe him money wch he lent yo^u owt of his
purce   I pray yo^u lett him haue it/ out of suche money as one
Mr Arnold is to paye yo^u/ No qd he he gettes no money of me
except he can wyn it by lawe/ and then this depo^t told him he
had A hard conscience.

Understanding that Inigo and another Spaniard "who
remayned for the most part at Padstow in the west
Cuntrye" had made a like false oath for countrymen of
theirs, Holmes asked his attorney to find out the truth of
the matter.   Kitchen

lerned by sondrye degrees that it was true indede/ and that the
frendes of the said Enegro had procured A Bull or pardon for him
& his said Cuntryman from the Pope for ther absolucion & re-
mission of ther periurye/ And that both the said Bull or pardone
& other popishe bookes coming by see vnto them were taken
vpon the See w^tin iij or iiij myles of the place where they duelt
and were broght to the Erll of Bedforde, wch being known to the
said Enegro, he ffled to london/ And then this depo^t made humble Sute to the said Erll to know whether it was so/ or not.

The Earl of Bedford told him it was true and that he had
granted warrants for their apprehension; and if the Earl
had not died shortly after (in 1585) Kitchen would have
procured his certificate to the Lords Chief Justices, before whom the cause then depended at Westminster Hall.
Kitchen charged Inigo in the King's Bench with the pardon
or bull, "And that yf it could be broght to light it wold
make him sweat."

Dr. Hector Nuñez, whom Kitchen accused of subornation of perjury, lived in 1582 in the same parish as Alonso
de Basurto, that of Allhallows Staynings.[1]   Inigo de Bal-

1. E 179/251/16.

derano, merchant stranger of the age of sixty, gave his residence as Padstow in Cornwall when he deposed in Chancery in 1589.[1] Corsino's witnesses also included Thomas de Madariaga, merchant of London, aged twenty-eight, and Robert Daborne of London, haberdasher, aged thirty-eight on November 29, 1589, the father of Robert Daborne the dramatist. He and John Achelley had appraised the goods of George Holmes at his house in Botolph Lane, after his death. The rich merchant Paul Bayning testifies that he was partner with George for "Trade in the levand Sees for the dominione of the Seignorie of Venis," and mentions George's ventures to Barbary. Corsino's bill[2] declares that the debt due him arose from a partnership in 1580 for "merchandize to be sent into Spayne"; that Thomas Holmes got his nephew Nicholas Holmes, a minor, to take out letters of administration; and that to defraud the creditors he "hathe or dothe intend to Convaye the said Nicolas into some foren Contry." Thomas retorts that Corsino himself remains in parts beyond the seas and is determined never to return into the realm.

By his detective work in tracing the papal bull granted to the Spaniard and in securing evidence of bribery by Dr. Nuñez, Kitchen proved himself an energetic and resourceful attorney. Thomas Holmes, of Borough Green, Cambridgeshire, esquire, for whom he was "Attournie or sollicitor," died in 1591. In a Chancery bill of November 6, 1602, Kitchen brought suit against the man who had married Holmes's widow, William Clarke of Chiveley, Cambridgeshire, yeoman. The printed calendar lists the plaintiff as "Richard Kechycie,"[3] but the original document

---

1. C 24/198, *ex parte* Corsino.   2. C 3/207/80.
3. *Calendar of the Proceedings in Chancery, in the Reign of Queen Elizabeth*, II (1830), 120.

reads "Richard Kechyne." [1] The bill relates that Nicholas Holmes of Bishop's Wearmouth, Durham, entrusted Kitchen with the letters of administration on the estate of his uncle, George Holmes, in order to recover "those debtes lyenge dyspersed in sundry places wherein yor pore Suppl^t hathe done his trewe & vttermoste endevo^r." Clarke secured the letters of administration and the *quietus est* by "solempnely vowinge" to return them faithfully within two days, which he failed to do. In consequence, Nicholas Holmes accused Kitchen of suppressing the letters and "Colludinge w^{t}h the Debto^{rs} & detractinge to prosecute suyte againste them," and threatened to call him before the judges. Clarke in his answer [2] offered to deliver the writings either to Nicholas or to the court, but not to Kitchen, who had seemed unwilling to hand them over "except he might haue some pece of monie geven him in regard of his kindnes to redeliuer the same," whereupon Clarke gave him money to satisfy his "Covetuous mynde." Kitchen, on the other hand, protested his "honeste & faythfull Care" to discharge his trust and to extend his utmost endeavor to recover the debts, in which he had spent great pains and travail and had never been paid even his expenses.

"Richard Kytchin of Cliffordes In gentleman of the age of xxxiiij yeres" testified again in Chancery on September 18, 1590, this time on behalf of Richard and Margaret Shepie against John Sweet.[3] Margaret was the daughter of another John Sweet of Calais, who had "A hed & beard of yellow or light aborne cullo^r," and her first husband was "a Damasker of Armo^r & weapons" of Calais, John Freemont,

1. C 2 Eliz. K 4/15.   2. C 2 Eliz. K 3/5.
3. C 24/203/89 (also numbered 73).

the old Earl of Arundel's armorer. I quote the testimony of George Boroughe of St. Botolph's without Bishopsgate, "burner of bones for the Quenes Ma^{tes} mynte in the To^r of london," an old man of eighty-six who says that he dwelt as a fisherman at Calais for thirty-six years before the town was lost (in 1558). Another witness was eighty-five years of age, Margaret, widow of Peter Johnson of St. Katherine's, cobbler. She "was then A Calyce woman borne & broght vppe in the same Towne," and "dwelled in Callyce by the space of l yeres or upward*es*, before Calice was lost, by the Myllegate in Brisket*tes* Rent*es* there/ foranempst one Mr Ratcliffe there/ that was some tyme Mayo^r of Callyce." Margaret remembers John Sweet as a soldier that kept the day-watch, "A tall handsome man w^t an Abron bearde & hedd," son of Robert Sweet that kept the day-watch, an Essex man from Prittlewell. Another Sweet, his uncle, she thinks, was porter of the gates of Calais. John's wife Florence "sold butter & chese," and she was one of those who lodged the retainers of Francis I at his meeting with Henry VIII at Calais in 1532.[1] John Swete was accused in 1539 of forging the will of John Senows, a priest.[2]

Richard Kitchen testified that certain copies of records perfectly agreed with the original court rolls, with which he had seen them examined. On September 29 "now shalbe three yeres he this depo^t being w^t one Tho. Pallmer in Prytillwell p*a*rishe in Essex" heard the defendant say that Shepie had been endeavoring to secure certain lands these sixteen years, "But ther be other landes wch in Right he

1. *Letters and Papers, Foreign and Domestic, of the Reign of Henry VIII*, V (1880), 628.
2. *Letters and Papers*, XIV, part II (1895), p. 371.

ought to haue." When Palmer asked for the rolls and writings, Sweet said, "I haue burnt them, and now lett him gett them of me aswell as he can by lawe, and w^t that he sayd, god be w^t yo^u, ffor I will never take him nor any of yo^u for my kynsman agayn." What Kitchen has to say about the case thus relates to the year 1587, when he visited the parish of Prittlewell (in which Southend is situated) at the mouth of the Thames. He had examined the court rolls of the manor of Prittlewell Priory, together with Geoffrey Thurgood of Rochford, "*serva*unt to the old lady Riche," the mother of Penelope Devereux's husband. Other witnesses in the case testify that stage plays used to be acted at Prittlewell on Whitsun Monday, "but ther hath none bene vsed there these xv yeres."

Kitchen's next deposition in Chancery concerns David Gittens, vintner, partner of Richard Smythe who in 1556 kept the Mermaid Tavern in Bread Street. The Vintners still own a Delft tankard bequeathed to the company, inscribed, "Thank David Gitting For Y^{is}." [1] "Rychard Keechin of g^t St Bartho*lom*ues nere Smythfielde london gent*leman* of the age of xxxiiij yeres" [2] deposed on April 15, 1591, that Katherine Johnson, daughter of David and Alice Gittens, told him "somewhat after Myche*lma*s last past in Bread strete" that among her mother's writings she had found Ireland's bond to Gittens for sixty pounds. She often told Kitchen that she would take no advantage of the bond for all the good in the world, because she thought in her conscience that it had long since been paid. "But qd she/ it was Mr Patenson in Sothwarke my husband*es* M^r/

1. Kenneth Rogers, *The Mermaid and Mitre Taverns in Old London* (1928), pp. 18, 19, 178–181.
2. C 24/ 221/41.

that advysed and caused her husband to put the said ob-
ligac*i*on in Sute against the comp^t And sayd that she had
cause to cursse the said Mr Patenson for setting her husband to suew the comp^t, who and his wyfe had bene more
like A father & mother vnto her/ then A frende." Her husband, however, said that he could take the money with a
safe conscience, because Ireland or his wife had received
privily as much or more from Alice Gittens; and he told
Kitchen that he sued on the bond in Yorkshire by Pattenson's advice in order to draw Ireland to compound with
him, though the bond was made in London. He had
secured for the trial an attorney dwelling in Yorkshire, one
Barker, and to follow the suit in the court of Common
Pleas "one Mr Danbye," an attorney of the Common
Pleas — possibly the William Danby who as coroner returned the inquest on Marlowe. Kitchen expresses his
opinion of such a proceeding: "he doth verelie think, ther
was some badd & hard mean*i*ng and practise to laye the sd
Acc*i*on to be tryed so farre of, considering all the parties to
that Sute had ther contynuall dwelling in london." This
was true, for John Ireland was assessed at sixty pounds in
1582 in the parish of St. Mildred's, Bread Street, where
David Gittens was also taxed; [1] while Johnson's master,
Brian Pattenson, was the leading vintner of Southwark
(warden of the Vintners' Company 1578-1580).[2] Examined in this suit, Pattenson gave his age as sixty. Ellis
Crispe, salter, employed by Ireland, repeated the statements of "Ry. keechin who shuld haue made an end of the
said matter by assent of both p*a*rties." Kitchen was thus

1. E 179/251/16.
2. Rogers, *The Mermaid and Mitre Taverns in Old London*, p. 182; *The Visitation of London in the Year 1568*, Harleian Society, I (1869), 63.

chosen as an impartial arbiter in October, 1589, the very month of his recognizance for Marlowe.

The four depositions in Chancery described above furnish nine instances of Kitchen's signature, which is a valuable means of distinguishing Marlowe's surety from other Richard Kitchens.   He signs himself "p me Ricum' (or Ric') Kechin," each time in the medieval court hand used in Queen's Bench and Common Pleas and therefore characteristic of attorneys at the common law.   The spelling shows how his surname was pronounced, as does also the Chancery clerk's constant spelling of the name as "Keechin."   The figures Kitchen gives for his age are thirty-five in February, 1588/9; thirty-one in January, 1589/90; and thirty-four in September, 1590, and in April, 1591.   In his Star Chamber testimony in June, 1600, he calls himself forty-six years of age.   From his own conflicting evidence the date of his birth may be put between 1554 and 1556, making him some eight or ten years older than Marlowe.

Further records of Kitchen's career as an attorney might be cited, but the above depositions are those closest in date to 1589, and they present samples of the variety of cases in which Kitchen was engaged at the time he knew Marlowe. In the first suit he was associated with his fellow-attorney Henry Trussell on behalf of a man whom his adversary called an extortioner, usurer, and cut-throat. In another he told how the Pope's pardon for the perjury of Inigo de Balderano was captured off the Cornish coast, and how the repentant Inigo cried "God mercy" in Kitchen's study at Clifford's Inn and swore that he was bribed by Dr. Hector Nuñez. In 1587 Kitchen traveled down the Thames, doubtless by water, to retrieve the Essex inheritance rightfully belonging to the daughter of a soldier in the garrison at Calais. Finally, in October, 1589, he was chosen to arbitrate between a rich merchant of Bread Street and a Southwark vintner's man concerning a bond made to a vintner in Bread Street, where we shall meet him once again in 1600.

The last deposition, in which Kitchen gives his address as Great St. Bartholomew's near Smithfield, proves beyond question that he was the Richard Kitchen found by Mr. Hotson paying five shillings subsidy on land in that parish in 1588 and by Mr. Brooke as the assailant of John Finch in the parish of Great St. Bartholomew's in 1594. Kitchen was indicted for this assault at the Guildhall on Thursday, April 11, 1594. One of the jurors was Baldwin Castleton, writer of the court letter, the master at this time of James Colbron, who next year became free and soon took as an apprentice John Milton the elder.[1] The jury of London citizens brought in the following indictment:[2]

quod Ricardus Kytchen nuper de London generoso secundo die Aprilis anno regni domine nostre Elizabethe Tricesimo sexto Apud London videlicet in parochia Sancti Bartholomei magni in Warda de ffarringdon extra London vi et armis videlicet Cultellis &c in quendam Johannem ffynche de London generosum in pace dei et dicte domine Regine adtunc et ibidem in parochia et Warda predictis ambulantem et existentem insultum et affraiam fecit Ac idem Ricardus Kytchen adtunc et ibidem cum vno pugione de ferro et calibi quem ipse in manu sua dextra habuit et tenuit eundem Johannem ffynche adtunc et ibidem verberauit vulnerauit et maletractauit Ita quod de vita sua desperabatur et alia enormia ei adtunc et ibidem intvlit ad grave dampnum et nocumentum ipsius Johannis ffynch et in omnium aliorum malefactorum pessimum et perniciosissimum exemplum Contra pacem dicte domine Regine Coronam et dignitatem suas &c/ Sebright.

1. David Masson, *The Life of John Milton*, I (1881), 26.
2. K. B. 9/685, m. 2.

Chief Justice Popham on May 13 issued a writ [1] commanding the justices of London to send into Queen's Bench all indictments against Richard Kytchyn for assaults and affrays, and the Lord Mayor and Alderman Martin accordingly returned the inquisition, which would not otherwise be preserved. Evidently Kitchen had secured a habeas corpus to remove his case from the court of the Mayor and Aldermen into Queen's Bench, where he himself was an attorney. In addition to the record which Mr. Brooke discovered among the Ancient Indictments, I find a later record of the prosecution in the Controlment Rolls.[2] An entry there inserted above Kitchen's name, "lib*eratur* hillar*ij* xxxviij° E*lizabethe* Regine," shows that the matter was finally discharged in 1595/6, almost two years after the affray.

Henslowe recorded in his diary that on August 9, 1598, he lent eight shillings and sixpence to Richard Alleyn, one of the players in his company, "to geue the atorney ceachen for the bande wch he hade in his hande." He also "Layd owt for hime the same time to m^r ceatchen" the sum of fifty shillings.[3] Dr. Greg asks, "Is the name an error for Cheacke?" — an attorney who had acted for Henslowe in 1593. Henslowe's spelling is erratic, but he is certainly trying to write the name Kechin or Kitchen. He is neither the first nor the last to spell it with a "C," for I find the name written "Chicthen" in a copy of a visitation of 1583 and "Citchin" in 1640.[4] Marlowe's friend signed his name "Kechin," and he was a practising attorney. There were

1. K. B. 9/685, m. 1.
2. K. B. 29/231, m. 70 dorso.
3. W. W. Greg, *Henslowe's Diary*, I (1904), 205; II (1908), 248.
4. Harleian MS. 1041, f. 72^v; *Calendars of Wills and Administrations at Lincoln*, IV, British Record Society, LVII (1930), 100.

also, however, an Anthony and a James Kitchen of Barnard's Inn.[1] "The atorney ceachen," therefore, cannot be
identified with certainty, but it is at least quite possible
that he was Richard Kitchen.

Finally, the most interesting record of Richard Kitchen
is his examination in Star Chamber on behalf of William
Williamson, host of the Mermaid in Bread Street.[2] On
June 1, 1600, "Richard Kitchin of the parish of St Giles
w^{t}howte criplegate gentel*man* adged fortie six yeres" testified as follows:

that aboute the time in this Inter*rogatory* menc*i*oned this depon^t
being walking w^{t}h will*i*am williamson in his house at the Meare-
mayde in Bred street Sr Edmond Baynehame Came in to the
sayd house vppon whose Coming the sayd [Sir Edmond Ba][3]
williamson sayd to this depon^t here is company Cominge in and
I had as lif haue they^r Roome as they^r company for they will
expect [that at my hand*es*][3] to haue musicke here and they shall
not haue any in my house & p^{r}sently after the sayd Sr Edmond
his comyng to the sayd house there Came twoe or three more of
the company thither wherof one of them sayd god*es* wound*es*
what shall we doe in this house for here we shall haue neyther
musick nor dicinge for the good man of this house is the precisest
man in Ingland and we had better haue gone to any Taverne in
london then to haue cume hither or word*es* to that effect and
sayeth that the sayd Sr Edmond and his sayd Company Came to
the sayd house to supper about vj of the clock in the yeevening
or some what after and presently the sayd williamson went from
this depon^t and tould him that he would goe to his men and giue
order that there should noe music*i*ons Cume vnto them w^{c}h is as
much as this depon^t remembreth to depose to this Inter*rogatory*.

The time mentioned in the interrogatory was the evening

1. Jeaffreson, *Middlesex County Records*, I, 192.
2. Star Chamber 5, A 1/29. Star Chamber records in the suit of Attorney
General v. Baynham and others are found also in A 43/37 and A 45/10.
3. Deleted.

of March 18, 1600. Kitchen was examined to the third interrogatory only, for he did not stay at the Mermaid as late
as eleven o'clock, when Baynham and his company left the
tavern in a merry mood and had several brushes with the
watchmen near St. Paul's. Kitchen's signature, which is
identical with that found in the Chancery depositions, es-
tablishes the fact that he was Richard Kitchen of Clifford's
Inn. That Marlowe's friend was also the friend of William
Williamson, "the precisest man in Ingland," speaks well
for his character. And since Kitchen knew the host of the
Mermaid, he must have known Shakespeare and Jonson as
well as Marlowe. His testimony that the Mermaid bore the
reputation of being an unusually quiet and respectable
tavern tends to confirm what William Beeston told
Aubrey, that Shakespeare was no company-keeper and
would not be debauched.[1] For the signature of William
Johnson of the Mermaid, examined on the same day as
Kitchen, proves that he was the William Johnson, vintner,
who acted as trustee for Shakespeare in 1613, and thus for
the first time furnishes evidence to corroborate the tradi-
tion of Shakespeare's connection with the Mermaid.

When Kitchen died in 1604, he left his house and closes
in Skipton, after the death of his wife Agnes, to the heirs
male of "Abell Kitchin of Bristow." His other kinsmen
lived far away in the dales of Yorkshire, but Abel Kitchen
was in London in 1604 as a commissioner sent to urge the
Crown officers to relieve Bristol from the obligation to pur-
vey wine, oil, and other foreign commodities.[2] Kitchen's
name was long preserved on one of the curious brass
posts in front of the Exchange in Bristol, erected as the

1. E. K. Chambers, *William Shakespeare* (1930), II, 252.
2. J. F. Nicholls and J. Taylor, *Bristol Past and Present*, I (1881), 272.

gift of Robert Kitchen by his four servants and executors, including Abel Kitchen. The executors also came to
the rescue of Bristol by a donation for the poor and the
building of a new market, when famine threatened the city
in the dear years of 1596 and 1597.[1] Robert Kitchen was
the mayor of Bristol who in 1589 sent up to the Council
Jeochim Gaunz, a Jewish mining engineer dwelling in the
Blackfriars, "a most wicked infidel, and not meet to be suf-
fered among Christians," because he denied the divinity of
the Saviour and declared, in a Hebrew conversation with a
minister, that God had neither wife nor child.[2] Robert
Kitchen's gifts to the poor of Bristol, Bath, and Kendal
in Westmorland (he was the son of Richard Kitchen of
Kendal) are commemorated in verse on a brass in St.
Stephen's church, and he left bequests in 1594 to Abel
Kitchen and to many other kinsmen, including Robert
Kitchen of London, merchant, son of his brother Richard.[3]

Abel Kitchen, to whose family Richard of Clifford's Inn
left his property, held office as sheriff of Bristol in 1599,[4]
warden of the Merchant Venturers in 1607, and master of
the company in 1610,[5] in which year one of the city council
was fined for using "very undecent and reproachful words"
to Mr. Kitchen at the election for mayor. Kitchen refused
a knighthood in 1631; [6] but the great event of his life was
his reception, as mayor of Bristol in 1613, of Queen Anne at

---

1. *Ibid.*, pp. 260-265.   2. S. P. Dom. Eliz. 226/40.
3. *A Chronicle of the Ancient and Noble Norman Family of De Havilland*
(1865), pp. 1, 63-66; Nicholls and Taylor, *Bristol Past and Present*, I, 261;
Waters, *Genealogical Gleanings in England*, I, 496 (and see II, 1097).
4. George Pryce, *A Popular History of Bristol* (1861), p. 184.
5. John Latimer, *The History of the Society of Merchant Venturers of the City
of Bristol* (1903), p. 326.
6. John Latimer, *The Annals of Bristol in the Seventeenth Century* (1900), pp.
41, 118.

her coming from Bath. In a scarlet gown, he welcomed her at the city gate and "presented to her Highness a fair purse of satten, embroidered with the two letters A. R. for her name, in which purse were 100 unites of gold, amounting to the summe of L. 110." After a marvelous show on the Severn in which one English ship fought and captured two Turkish galleys, Kitchen feasted the Queen's train at his house; "And then the Ladie Drummond did deliver unto Mr. Maior a fair ring of gold set with diamonds very richly, supposed to be worth L. 60, as a favour from the Queen's Majestie, which he wore next day about his neck, hung by a chain of gold." [1] By his will in 1639/40 [2] Kitchin left to his son Abel

my signett of gould and my chain of Gould and alsoe a gould Ringe sett with diamonds which ye Noble queene Queene Anne gave me at her beinge in Bristoll . . . And my Will is that my said Sonne Abell shall not sell that Ringe sett with Diamonds, But leave it to posteritie of our name in memorie as a guifte from soe noble a queene.

The ring, however, is said to have "mysteriously disappeared at his decease." [3] His son Abel, a barrister of the Middle Temple,[4] died within the year; but his descendants were still pensioned by the chamber of Bristol in 1824.[5] There are probably descendants living to-day who are the heirs of Marlowe's friend Richard Kitchen.

1. John Nichols, *The Progresses, Processions, and Magnificent Festivities of King James the First, his Royal Consort, Family, and Court* (1828), II, 643–666.

2. Prerogative Court of Canterbury, 109 Coventry. Administration was granted in August, 1640, to his daughter Mary Meredith, and in 1647 to her son Abel Meredith.

3. Nicholls and Taylor, *Bristol Past and Present*, I, 276.

4. C. T. Martin, *Minutes of Parliament of the Middle Temple*, II (1904), 658, 752.

5. Nicholls and Taylor, *Bristol Past and Present*, I, 276.

Humphrey Rowland, the other surety for Marlowe, is a less important person than Richard Kitchen. In "Marlowe among the Churchwardens" Mr. Hotson told how he found traces of Rowland in the Controlment Roll of Queen's Bench for 1586 (really 1585), in the subsidy list for 1598, and in the parish register of St. Botolph's, Aldgate. The register calls Rowland "horn-breaker," a word not to be found in *A New English Dictionary*. Mr. Hotson discusses the term in the following paragraph: [1]

Rowland's occupation, however, still remains a mystery. It some entries he is called a "horner," and in others a "horn-breaker." The first description offers no difficulty. A horner is one who prepares horn for human use in buttons, hornbooks, and the like. Little Jack Horner's progenitor was one such. But is this equivalent to "horn-breaking"? I do not know. Horn-breaking — what is it? Rehabilitation of cuckolds? Manual dehorning of cattle? If this latter be the case, what a Samson our Rowland must have been! A Tamburlaine of tradesmen.

The mystery of Rowland's trade is solved by two letters preserved at the Guildhall, one from Burghley and the other a reply by the Lord Mayor. Burghley wrote the following letter on Rowland's behalf:

After my very hartie comendacions to your good L[p] whereas this bearer Humfrie Rowland a very honest poore man hath obtained the consent and good willes of the Companie of the Cutlers to be free of their companie, if so be he might obteine the assent and liking of yo[r] L[p] and the Aldermen. In respect of the honestie of the man, and credible report of his skill and his facultie I ame the more willing to recommend him and his suite to yo[r] L[ps]. good fauor and respect, prayeng yo[w] very hartely at this my request, to yelde him your owne, and to obteine for him the consent[es] of the rest of the aldermen, so that together with

1. *The Atlantic Monthly*, CXXXVIII (1926), 44.

his graunt alredie of the companie of the cutlers he may receue his freedome, for wch your L^ps goodnesse toward him besides that I shall thanke yow, the poore man and his shall euer be bound to pray for yo^w And so I bid your L^p hartely farewell ffrom Westminster this xij^th of June 1583.

The Lord Mayor specifies Rowland's trade in replying to his "singular good L. the Lord high tresorer of England":

My dutie humbly done to yor L^p. Vpon receipt of yor honor-able le*tt*res in fauo^r of Humfrie Rowland maker of Lanterne hornes to be admitted into the fredome of this citie in the companie of cutlers which art he doth not occupie: albeit it be against the ordinances of the citie that any shold be made free by gift but in the art w^e he vseth: I and my brethren were neuerthelesse redie in mindfulnesse of yor continuall fauo^r to this citie to haue don what laie in vs for satisfieng yor request. The companie of horners, who in dede are a verie pore comipanie and greatly de-caied, hearing of that suit of Rowland, haue exhibited to vs their peti*ci*on in articles for staie of such admission, which bicause it is the complaint of a companie of pore citisens, and maie conteine mater whereof yor L^p was not before informed, I haue sent the articles herew^th to yor L^p and willed the said wardens to attend vpon yo^w, for iustifieng of their bill, and for answering such maters as yor L^p in that behalf shall require to be satisfied. And so I humbly leaue to troble yor L^p. At London this last of June. 1583.[1]

Rowland, then, was a worker in horn, and especially a "maker of Lanterne hornes" — very necessary articles in the black, unlit streets of Elizabethan London. But the horn he broke went to the making of other products as well. The fact that the Cutlers were willing to take him into their

1. Remembrancia, I, nos. 505, 516 (fols. 256, 262); summarized by W. H. and H. C. Overall, *Analytical Index to the Series of Records Known as the Remembrancia* (1878), p. 154.

company, though he did not practise their art, suggests that they had dealt with him in their trade, probably buying from him such articles as the horn handles of knives. The Barber-Surgeons' Company took a fancy to another of his products. For on September 29, 1586, the company granted him a lease of a house in East Smithfield, at the rent of six pounds a year, on condition that he deliver to the masters of the company, when they came every year to view the property, "the nombre of xviij shoing hornes franck and ffree." [1]

In the churchwardens' accounts of St. Botolph, Aldgate, "Humphrey Roland hornebreaker of the maner of East Smithfield" sets down his account in 1584 as one of the two renters of the lands belonging to the parish. The registers of St. Botolph show that Rowland was the father of a large family. "Edmound Rollaund Sonne vnto Humphrey rolaund" was christened on November 7, 1571. Other children followed at intervals of two years: Ellen on August 30, 1573; Agnes on December 18, 1575; Mary on September 22, 1577; and Simon on October 28, 1579. [2] Mr. Hotson printed the burial entries for several of these children: Ann (probably the same as Agnes) on December 7, 1577; and on September 30, 1582, Ellen and Simon, who both died of the plague. I find "Phinees Rollaund sonne vnto Humphrey Rollaund hornnebreaker" christened on December 22, 1583. Further records of the family were also printed by Mr. Hotson, including the burial of Rowland's wife Mary on February 27, 1585. Rowland married Eve Ashe on May 4 following. Thirteen days after the wedding his

1. Sidney Young, *The Annals of the Barber-Surgeons of London* (1890), p. 188. My friend Mr. Bernard M. Wagner pointed out to me both the above references to Rowland's occupation.
2. These entries were found by my friend Mr. J. W. Bowman.

sister, Amy Skriwater, widow, was buried, "Yeres 38. *consumption*." By his second wife Rowland had Elizabeth, christened on May 14, 1587. But "Samwell Rollaund," christened on July 20, 1589, was buried at the age of "1. yere. 3 quarters. pyning," and his brother Godfrey was buried on August 23, 1593, "Yeres 2. plagg."

Of Rowland's numerous servants, Mr. Hotson found entries of the burial in 1577 of James Paadge; in 1583 of Andrew Vandepeare, who died of consumption at the age of sixteen; and in 1593 of Awsten Awstens. A certificate in 1581 of strangers "which are of no church" names "Jnᵒ Carpenter and Jnᵒ Cornelis, of Andwerp, servantes to Humfrye Roland, in Estsmithfeild."[1] The subsidy roll for Portsoken Ward in 1600 lists among the aliens in East Smithfield "Symon Symerie servaunt to Humphrie Rowland."[2]

Marlowe's recognizance in 1589 is by no means Rowland's only appearance in the Middlesex Sessions Rolls. He was one of the two constables for East Smithfield in 1581, and he still held office in 1584 and 1585.[3] He gave bail for two other persons beside Marlowe. On July 16, 1584, he was one of the unusual number of five sureties required for Elizabeth, wife of Bartholomew Clevener, a tailor of East Smithfield, who made her appearance and was committed to prison.[4] As Humphrey "Roland," of East Smithfield, horner, he was surety on April 13, 1591, for Robert Gill of East Smithfield, vintner, bound over to keep the peace toward his own wife. Gill's tavern, I find, was

1. R. E. G. Kirk and E. F. Kirk, *Returns of Aliens, The Publications of the Huguenot Society of London*, X, ii (1902), 219.

2. Kirk, *Returns of Aliens*, X, iii (1907), 80.

3. Sessions Rolls 231/16, 252/29, 258/11.

4. Sessions Roll 252/89 (cf. no. 33).

the Castle in East Smithfield.[1] Jury lists of April, 1592, and December, 1593, contain the name of Humphrey Rowland, but he was not among those sworn.[2] Sir Owen Hopton on August 1, 1591, accepted the bond of Rowland alone, without surety, that he would appear at the Sessions of the Peace, under a penalty of ten pounds, "to answer to such things as shall be objected against him on the part of the Queen."[3] Recognizances thus phrased frequently mean that the person in question was bound over for victualing or keeping an alehouse without license. The clerk records that Rowland came and was discharged.

Some minor breach of the law probably occasioned the entry which Mr. Hotson found in the Controlment Rolls:[4]

Middlesex ss venire facias octabis hillarij humfridum Rowland de parochia de Estsmythfelde in Comitatu Middlesex yoman respondere Regine de quibusdam transgressis & extorcionibus vnde indicatus est — per Bagam supradictam.

The date of the entry is Michaelmas term, 28 Elizabeth — 1585, not 1586; and a note over Rowland's name adds that he was outlawed in the following Hilary term (1585/6). James and Helen Browne of St. Botolph's, Bishopsgate, were likewise indicted for "trespasses and extortions." Rowland's offense was not necessarily serious. The next entry records the indictment of Sir Rowland Heyward, the senior alderman of London, for encroaching on the highway in Hackney; and on the recto of the same membrane are indictments of two neighbors of Rowland, John Edwards and John Grosse, for not repairing the street at

1. Sessions Roll 296/44; Bodleian MS. top. Berks. d. 12, f. 183.
2. Sessions Rolls 306/6, 318/106.
3. Sessions Roll 300/12.
4. K. B. 29/222, m. 12 dorso.

East Smithfield. A number of victualers were indicted for allowing unlawful games, contrary to the statute for the maintenance of archery; among them were Robert Miles of Whitechapel (whom Richard Burbage next year beat with a broom-staff at the Theater) and Baptist Starr, the constable of Ratcliffe, who was also outlawed. Rowland was summoned to appear on the same day as William Byrd, the greatest of English musicians, indicted as a Catholic recusant, and Sir Fulk Greville of Warwickshire (the father of Sidney's friend), who had found buried treasure on his land and was forced to pay it in to the Queen.[1]

Rowland's trespass did not prevent his election as churchwarden of St. Botolph, Aldgate. I find some very interesting records copied in a manuscript at the Bodleian [2] from an old parish record book (which I have also used for verification). A vestry meeting on December 11, 1586, agreed "that Humphrey Rollaunde shalbe churche warden according to the olde Custom for too yers if God permit." [3] On January 19, 1586/7, the "Churchwardens and sydesmen ded keepe there visitation dinner at ye Signe of ye thre tonnes as we go towards ye mineries." The cost of the dinner for twenty-five persons was twenty-six shillings and tenpence, toward which the parish allowed twenty shillings and Rowland contributed eightpence. Important events of 1587, such as Sidney's funeral, are carefully recorded in the churchwardens' book. "Memorandum," runs an entry of February 9, "that we ded ringe at oure parishe churche and was for ioye that the Queene of Skotts that enemye to ower most noble Queen maiestie and ower

1. K. B. 29/222, membranes 2 dorso, 11 dorso.
2. Bodleian MS. top. Berks. d. 12.
3. Bodleian MS., f. 135.

contrie was beheaded ffor the which the Lord God be praysed." [1]

As churchwarden Rowland was one of the leaders in the yearly perambulation of the parish bounds. The procession marched from Whitechapel Bars to Sparrow's Corner and down Hog Lane, through the Well Close and down Nightingale Lane (where John Wolfe planned to build a playhouse in 1600). At the mill the parishioners sang the Hundredth Psalm, then proceeded through St. Katherine's and along by the Iron Gate of the Tower till the under-porter of the Tower, attended by three warders with halberds on their shoulders, forbade them in the Queen's name to go farther. The dramatic appearance of the officers of the Tower often thus prevented the parishioners from claiming what they considered their ancient boundaries; but in 1588, the churchwardens record, their procession met no resistance. The visitation dinner in that year was held at the sign of the Harrow in "Gratius street," and the "Biden gess" at the feast included "Mownsure Cranes wyfe and another Kindsman of Humphrie Rowlands." The twenty-seven who sat down to dinner not only ate an abundance of beef and chicken, and six rabbits, but they drank three gallons of claret, two pottles of sack, and two quarts of Malmsey, beside indulging in the luxury of "orrenges at x d.," so that the whole dinner cost forty-seven shillings. Next year, when the dinner cost only twenty-five shillings, Rowland and his wife were again at the banquet. [2]

Rowland did not often go to law, but I have found him as a defendant in Star Chamber. [3] The dramatist Fletcher's father, as Almoner to the Queen, entered a bill on Novem-

<hr>

1. Bodleian MS., fols. 172–174.   2. Bodleian MS., fols. 176–182.
3. Star Chamber 5, A 50/11.

ber 6, 1594, against Richard Swift, Humphrey Rowland, and William Sutton, the last two as executors of Robert Bowers, gun-maker. By his will of September, 1591, Bowers had instructed Rowland and Sutton to pay the money he owed as trustee to William English of Bermondsey and to Richard Swift, his fellow-trustee for English. Swift, a Bermondsey fellmonger or leatherseller, testified in Star Chamber that he "wholy relyed vppon theire faythfull and iust meanyng," he being "altogether vnlyttered." [1] He recovered against Rowland and Sutton in the Queen's court of St. Katherine's, and received the rents due him as surviving trustee, being "layabell" to English in "A good Round some." On April 6, 1594, English became "felone de see" (*felo-de-se*) by hanging himself. Bishop Fletcher accordingly claimed all rents due to the suicide as deodands. Swift declared in his answer that English was only fifteen years old when he killed himself, and therefore too young to hold title to the rents. Rowland and Sutton on November 24 entered a joint and several answer, signed by their counsel "Emylie" — Thomas Emylie of Northamptonshire, sued in 1596 by the poet Spenser, his wife Elizabeth, and her brothers George and Alexander Boyle. [2]

"Humphrie Rowlande" paid a tax of eight shillings on goods assessed at three pounds in the subsidy roll for East Smithfield, October 31, 1598. [3] If his income had been any less, he would not have been on the subsidy roll at all. In fact, he is not listed in 1600. His later years were not prosperous, though he continued to take part in the parish business of St. Botolph, Aldgate, as "Mr. Humphrey Row-

1. Star Chamber 5, A 46/12.   2. C 2 Eliz. S 1/40.
3. E 179/142/239; cited by Mr. Hotson.

land." As "Humphrey Rowland a horne breaker" he was buried, I find, on January 14, 1600/1. The decline of his fortunes is shown by the fact that when his widow Eve — the Eve Ashe he had married in 1585 — exhibited an inventory on January 26, the whole estate came to only thirty-five shillings, and she thereupon renounced the administration.[1]

Since several of Rowland's servants were Dutch, and two of them were from Antwerp, it would be interesting to know whether he was related to Richard Rowlands, generally known as Verstegen from the surname he used in Antwerp and under which he published *The Restitution of Decayed Intelligence in Antiquities concerning the English Nation* (Antwerp, 1605). The antiquary was born in the parish of St. Katherine's, adjoining East Smithfield, son of a cooper and grandson of Theodore Roland Verstegen, an exile from Holland.[2] Several coopers named Rowland lived in East Smithfield, and the constable of the precinct in 1600 and later years was Samuel Rowland or Rowlands, churchwarden in 1619, who died in 1626.[3] It is not impossible that he was Samuel Rowlands the author, of whose personal history absolutely nothing is known. The dates correspond very well, for Rowlands made his appearance as an author in 1598 and his exit with a book which was licensed in 1627/8 but may have been written somewhat earlier, after which he disappears from sight.

The strangest thing about Humphrey Rowland is that Marlowe should have been associated with him at all. The maker of lantern horns seems to have led a comparatively

1. Archdeaconry of London, Act Book 3, f. 140ᵛ.
2. See the *D.N.B.* under "Rowlands *alias* Verstegen, Richard."
3. Archdeaconry of London, Act Book 6, f. 27ᵛ.

uneventful life, and as constable and churchwarden he was an orthodox member of society. Perhaps, indeed, he had done some special service to merit the intervention of Burghley in his favor in 1583; but, on the other hand, the Lord Treasurer may merely have been willing to do a good turn to one of the Middlesex constables. Even conjecture is hard pressed to imagine how Marlowe is likely to have made his acquaintance. Mr. Hotson suggested that they became acquainted "through a wealthy coparishioner of Rowland's named James Morley or Morlowe, perhaps a distant kinsman of Christopher Marlowe." James Morlowe, Mr. Hotson pointed out, is assessed in East Smithfield in 1586, and James Morley and Thomas Morley in 1598. These records refer, however, to two James Morleys, father and son, and the father makes no mention of the name Marlowe in his will, proved on September 9, 1592.[1] From a Chancery deposition of 1593 I find that James Morley the elder did not live in East Smithfield, but "dwelled & dyed in Grenewiche." He was a London ironmonger who became rich enough to buy property in Kent and in East Smithfield, which he leased out to tenants such as Derrick Newark, a Dutch cooper.[2] Morley gave his name to his grandson Sir James Bourchier, whose daughter Elizabeth married "Oliver Cromwell, alias Williams, of Huntingdon, esq." Cromwell assured his wife's jointure in 1620 to Thomas Morley, citizen and leatherseller, the Thomas assessed in 1598, his brother Isaac Morley being a witness.[3] There is no evidence that the Morleys were re-

1. Prerogative Court of Canterbury, 72 Harrington.
2. C 24/235/21; H. H. Drake, *Hasted's History of Kent*, part I (1886), 207.
3. Mark Noble, *Memoirs of the Protectoral-House of Cromwell* (1787), I, 123, 124, 132.

lated in any way to Christopher Marlowe, and they may therefore be dismissed from further consideration.

Possibly it was Richard Kitchen who secured Rowland to go bail with him for his client Marlowe. For Kitchen's wife had a brother James Redman, "a scrivener or schoolmaster" who dwelt near Sparrow's Corner in East Smithfield.[1] Kitchen must, therefore, have had acquaintances in East Smithfield. Redman was not on the subsidy list, but he would know which of his neighbors were, and one of his neighbors was Humphrey Rowland. Rowland, who had been churchwarden of the parish for two years, was an eminently respectable surety. When Marlowe needed bail to deliver him from Newgate, he probably got into touch with Richard Kitchen; and the energetic Kitchen may well have arranged the whole affair for him. Kitchen, who in 1600 was the familiar acquaintance of the host of the Mermaid Tavern, was a man of education and intelligence. He is much more likely than Rowland to have been a friend of Marlowe.

1. Bodleian MS. top. Berks. d. 12, f. 185.

CHAPTER V

Marlowe and the Constables

THE fray in Hog Lane was not the only occasion which brought Marlowe into collision with the law. I have had the good fortune to come upon still another record of a definite event in the otherwise wholly conjectural history of his life in London. Once more it is to be found in the Sessions Rolls at the Middlesex Guildhall in Westminster.

The document in question is a recognizance entered into by Marlowe alone, and the best introduction to it will be the well-weighed remarks of Jeaffreson in summing up his long labors on this very numerous class of records: [1]

From nine out of every ten recognizances, all that can be learnt is that nine humble and obscure persons, whose names are in no way associated with any matter of present interest, were ordered under more or less heavy penalties to keep the peace towards their neighbours, to desist from committing some commonplace nuisance, or to appear at some future Gaol-Delivery or Session of Peace, for the purpose of answering to some accusation, or of giving evidence tending to prove some quite obscure person guilty of some utterly unhistoric offence. The majority of the persons, thus bound over by recognizances of no historic moment, were mechanics who had beaten their wives or their neighbours' wives, labourers who had come to blows over too many pots of heady ale, artisans guilty of jeering at the constables, young tailors or other young craftsmen guilty

1. *Middlesex County Records*, I, xlviii f.

of presuming to set up in business on their own account, instead of working as journeymen for masters entitled to their services, apprentices with heads broken in a recent riot, women at war with women of their street or yard, petty tradesmen accused of paltry frauds, householders charged with obstructing a common sewer, or persons suspected of victualling without a licence.

Under no circumstances could the recognizances of such people and their sureties be diverting or usefully instructive: but these writings are especially barren and unprofitable, on account of their silence respecting the very particulars about which one would wish them to be most communicative. . . .

In dealing with these documents, the majority of which are as unentertaining and historically worthless as several thousands of ancient writings can well be, I persisted in my resolution to examine every one of them. Had I been less persistent in a labour, not altogether fruitless of good though inexpressibly tedious, I might have missed the important recognizance, taken on 19 Dec., 20 Eliz., which revealed the important fact, that, instead of kneeling before his sovereign for the first time in the year 1582, as his successive biographers have represented, Walter Raleigh was a bright feature of Elizabeth's court as early as 1577, — a fact which, on its being communicated promptly to Professor Gosse, enabled that fine and subtle critic to perfect one of the most remarkable demonstrations of recent literary research.

Jeaffreson spoke from experience, and I can endorse all that he says about these provokingly close-mouthed bits of parchment. His account has naturally not allured other enquirers to examine for themselves the formidable array of volumes containing the Middlesex Sessions records. And yet, though unentertaining to the general reader, no body of unique documents can ever be historically worthless. Most recognizances tell little or nothing in themselves of what has brought the maker before a justice of the peace. None the less, each has its story, and one who has cultivated acquaintances among the men and women of a particular period sometimes finds it possible to put together the fragments of scattered records so that they tell us more than each would apart. Such has proved to be the case with Marlowe's first recognizance. The same is true of several recognizances in 1598 of persons bound to keep the peace toward Matthew Roydon, who has himself told the history of the preceding events very fully and dramatically in pleadings, still preserved, in the court of Star Chamber. At other times, as in the second appearance of Marlowe before the Middlesex Sessions, the recognizance stands alone, and from it we must draw all that we are likely to know about the culprit's brush with the law.

No one person can possibly notice all the items of interest among a multitude of records, and it is not surprising that Jeaffreson passed without notice over many as important as those he summarized. In making a thorough search of all the extant Sessions files for the latter part of Elizabeth's reign and the first half of James I's, I have met with a number of appearances before the justices by Thomas Dekker, George Wilkins, Anthony Munday, and other poets and playwrights, all of which records I shall elsewhere describe in full. Among the thousands of recognizances which Jeaffreson dismissed as of no historic moment are the two which throw light on a greater poet even than Raleigh: that of 1589, which he calendared without realizing that "Christopher Marley" was Marlowe; and another of May 9, 1592, which he omitted, endorsed "Christofer Marle his Recognizance."

Under this effectual disguise of a variant spelling we find the last trace of Marlowe before he left play-writing, for six weeks later the theaters were closed by the Privy Council's inhibition. The record runs as follows:

Middlesex ss Memorandum quod ix^no die Maij 1592 Annoque Regni domine nostre Elizabethe Nunc &c xxxiiij^to Venit coram me Owino Hopton Milite vno Justiciariorum dicte domine Regine ad pacem in comitatu predicto Conservandam assignatorum Christopherus Marle de London generosus et recognovit se debere dicte domine Regine xx^li bone et legalis monete Anglie: Sub Condicione quod personaliter comparebit ad proximam generalem Sessionem pacis in et pro comitatu predicto tenendam: et interim geret pacem versus cunctum populum dicte domine Regine et precipue versus Allenum Nicholls Constabularium de Hollowellstreet in comitatu predicto et Nicholaum Helliott subconstabularium de eadem:/ Quam summam predictam concessit de bonis et Cattallis terris atque tenementis suis ad vsum dicte domine Regine per formam Recognicionis levari Si defecerit in premissis &c ^1

The document just quoted is not among the Gaol Delivery files, like the previous memorandum, but among the records for the General Session of the Peace to be held at Westminster after Michaelmas, 1592. In the other shires of England the justices were required by statute to hold Quarter Sessions, in January, after Easter, in June, and in October; but since Middlesex freeholders had to serve on juries in all the high courts at Westminster, and since the Gaol Deliveries at Newgate dealt with the principal offenses in Middlesex as well as in London, the statute of 14 Henry VI, c.4, dispensed the magistrates from holding more than two General Sessions a year. They were always kept in the first week after Michaelmas and the first week after the close of Easter.^2 In 1592 Easter fell on March 26,

1. Sessions Roll 309, no. 13.
2. Jeaffreson, *Middlesex County Records*, I, xx ff.

and when Marlowe was taken up in May for his threats against the constables, the next Sessions were five months away. Of the other recognizances in the file only one dates from May, two date from June, and the rest from later months. Two neighbors of Marlowe were bound on October 3 to keep the peace reciprocally: Nicholas Tomson of Hollowell Street, victualer, for whom John Banes of Shoreditch, victualer, acted as a surety, to keep the peace towards Stephen Watkyns, and Stephen Watkyns of Hollowell Street, "Tealer," to keep the peace towards Nicholas Tomson. Marlowe's is in the usual form for such documents; but while most of the others bear a later memorandum that the recognitor made his appearance as required, no such note has been entered for Marlowe.

When we next hear of Marlowe after the seizure of Kyd's papers in May a year later, the Council is ordering him arrested at the house of Mr. Thomas Walsingham in Kent. The plague had broken out in August, 1592. Greene on his deathbed after his drinking-bout with Nashe had called upon "those Gentlemen his Quondam acquaintance, that spend their wits in making plaies," above all on Marlowe, the "famous gracer of Tragedians," entreating their "rare wits to be imploied in more profitable courses."[1] In the summer, therefore, Marlowe was probably still in London, hoping that plays would begin again when the inhibition ended at Michaelmas. The plague, however, put an end to such hopes. If he spent part of his last year of life at Scadbury, writing *Hero and Leander*, he may not have been at hand when the time came to appear at the General Sessions in October. He would be liable for the twenty pounds of his recognizance until he

1. *Greenes Groats-Worth of Witte* (1592), signatures E 4ᵛ–F 1ᵛ.

had discharged it, but the forfeiture would be difficult to collect while he remained in Kent, and if he had left Holywell Street the endangered constables might rejoice to be rid of him without further trouble.

The Michaelmas Sessions of 1592 at which Marlowe should have made his appearance were held in October before Sir Owen Hopton, Gabriel Goodman, Matthew Dale, John Barnes, Jerome Hawley, Serjeant Fleetwood, Christopher Rythe, John Haynes, Richard Young, and three other Middlesex justices.[1] Goodman was the Dean of Westminster who befriended Camden and contributed material and verses to the *Britannia*. Young was the most active of the justices in hunting down Catholics. In 1589, for example, a Mrs. Dewse heard that Robert Birche was a conjurer and solicited him to make pictures of wax of her enemies and then prick them to the heart. The enemies of whom she thus desired to be revenged were Sir Rowland Heyward, Recorder Fleetwood, and "that thief, Justice Younge, who lived by robbing Papists." [2]

To the Middlesex justices belonged the duty of supervising the public playhouses north of the Thames, since neither the Theater nor the Curtain was within the City's jurisdiction. Accordingly, in the month following Marlowe's binding over to the peace, it was to the Master of the Rolls (Sir Gilbert Gerrard), Sir Owen Hopton, John Barnes, and Richard Young that the Council addressed its letters of June 23, 1592, ordering them to set a strong watch on Midsummer Eve and Night for the avoiding of such tumults as had arisen earlier in June in Southwark.

---

1. Sessions Roll 309, no. 69.
2. S. P. Dom. Eliz. 230/30, 31; G. L. Kittredge, *Witchcraft in Old and New England* (1929), pp. 89, 419; Chambers, *The Elizabethan Stage*, I, 285.

Moreover, the justices were to prevent any plays from being performed at the Theater, Curtain, or other usual places, "nor no other sorte of unlawfull or forbidden pastymes that drawe togeather the baser sorte of people." The Council register merely notes that like letters were sent to the officers of the liberties and to Gardiner and the other justices for Surrey.[1] Mr. Hotson records these letters solely as providing against riots,[2] but they must have included orders to close the Rose and Paris Garden, an equal source of danger with the Shoreditch playhouses, especially since Southwark had been the center where the apprentices of Blackfriars and Bermondsey had chosen to assemble under pretext of going to see a play.   Justice Gardiner, therefore, had been charged with the duty of suppressing plays on the Bankside several years before his quarrel with Langley and the later order of the Council to pluck down the Swan. The experience probably gave him confidence that authority would be on his side in any encounter with such dealers in forbidden pastimes as Langley and Shakespeare.

Before leaving "Christofer Marle his Recognizance," it may be well to satisfy our minds whether there is any reasonable ground for doubting that "Christofer Marle" is the poet. Until Mr. Hotson published his discoveries, the only contemporary Christopher who had ever been unearthed was a Christopher Marlowe of the Canterbury district, who lived into the seventeenth century and was presented in an Archdeacon's Visitation.[3] Mr. Hotson showed that the Christopher Morley of the Council's

1. *Acts of the Privy Council,* XXII (1901), 549.
2. *Shakespeare versus Shallow,* p. 254.
3. Ingram, *Christopher Marlowe and his Associates.* p. 13.

letter to Cambridge was the dramatist and not Christopher
Morley of Trinity, who had already taken his M. A. in
1586. Sir Israel Gollancz adduced evidence of a "Christopher Marlowe *alias* Mathews" imprisoned in the Gate-
house in 1604, the man whom William Vaughan had reported two years before as going under the name of
"Christopher Marlor." He entered the Jesuit college at
Valladolid as "John Matthew al*ias* Christopher Marler,"
aged twenty-seven in 1599, three years after he also had
taken his M. A. at Trinity, Cambridge, under his true
name of Matthews.[1] He cannot have been the "Marle"
of 1592, and there is no record of the earlier Morley's
being in London.

These, however, were by no means the only men contemporary with the poet who bore the name of Christopher
Marlowe or Morley. I have found several others in London
alone, and these are more to our present purpose than the
Cambridge Masters of Arts. They ought to be carefully
kept in mind if we are to avoid possible sources of confusion.

In the first place, the register of St. Mary Abchurch
contains the following entry: "Mr Christopher Marloe
buried the thirde of January," 1576/7. His will, however,
proved four days later, shows that his real name was
Marler. Citizen and merchant tailor of London, he was
a Yorkshire man by origin. He appointed as executor
"my cosen, Mr Thomas Jennyson, the Queenes Majesties
auditor in Ireland," a Durham squire who was to disinherit
as a Catholic his son William, the friend of Thomas Lodge.

---

1. Cf. Boas, *Marlowe and his Circle*, pp. 18-21. The records have now been
published by Canon Edwin Henson in *Registers of the English College at Valladolid*, Catholic Record Society, XXX (1930), 57 (cf. p. 46 n.).

Marler left twelvepence to each inhabitant of St. Mary
Abchurch who would accept it, and appointed to have
the keeping of his money his well-beloved friend Mr. Richard Young.[1] This was evidently the active priest-hunter
mentioned above, the justice also who informed Puckering
in June, 1593, of the arrest of Cholmley for the opinions
Marlowe had instilled in him. The register gives us the
date of the burial of "Mr Richard Yeoung Esquier" as
December 15, 1594, recording also the burial of a "Richard
Banes merchauntailo^r" on February 6, 1596/7. "Xpofer
Marlowe" and Richard Young were each assessed at fifty
pounds in the subsidy roll for St. Mary Abchurch in
1563/4.[2]

Closer to the poet in time is an entry which occurs in
the register of St. Vedast's, Foster Lane, two years after
Robert Herrick was christened there:[3]

X'pofer Morley, s'vant to William Beale, was buried the xiith
day of September 1593.

He probably died of the plague, which Gabriel Harvey
supposed to have carried off Marlowe that same summer;
for a fellow-servant received burial two days earlier and
his master's daughter Rachaell eleven days afterward.

In the parish of St. James, Clerkenwell, there evidently
lived more than one Christopher Morley. "Thomas son
of Xpofer Morley" was christened on June 24, 1571.
Christopher Morley married Elizabeth Curwin in 1594,
and one of the same name married Susan Pound in 1602.
Susan, wife of Christopher, was buried in 1603, as was also

---

1. Prerogative Court of Canterbury, 1 Daughtry, mentioned by Brooke, *The
Life of Marlowe*, p. 2, and summarized in *North Country Wills*, II (Surtees Society, CXXI, 1912), 81.
2. E 179/145/218.
3. *Harleian Society Registers*, XXX (1903), 140.

an Owen Morley, son of Christopher, while Elizabeth, wife of Christopher, lived until 1618. A Christopher Morley married in 1620 and was perhaps the Christopher who had a daughter Thomazen christened in 1626.[1] Thus we have a man of the name living in 1571 (considerably older than Marlowe) and three subsequent marriages by a Christopher. Some of these were probably remarriages, but even so the evidence points to at least two or three men of this name living in Clerkenwell.

The most interesting of all the Christophers is "Christopher s. of Thomas Morley, gentleman, and Suzan his wife," baptized on June 26, 1599, at St. Helen, Bishopsgate.[2] He was the son of Thomas Morley the famous madrigalist, whose "It was a lover and his lass" has been called the ideal of what a Shakespearian setting ought to be, and who in the year of Christopher's birth published in his *Consort Lessons* the lovely music of "O Mistress Mine."

I find in the Middlesex Sessions files one more record, beside those already discussed, which deals with a Christopher Morley of Elizabeth's reign. On November 19, 1602, William Vernam of St. James, Clerkenwell, laborer, entered bond in ten pounds to give evidence and prefer a bill of indictment, at the next Sessions of Peace to be held at the Castle in St. John Street, against "Christoferum morley" of St. Sepulchre's without Newgate, carpenter, for suspicion of felony.[3] The Sessions records tell nothing more except that Vernam came as he had promised.

Still another previously unnoticed Christopher Morley died in the plague year of 1603. "In the name of God,

---

1. *Harleian Society Registers*, IX (1884), 6, 104; XIII (1887), 18, 26, 49; XVII (1891), 82, 83, 140.
2. *Ibid.*, XXXI (1904), 8.   3. Sessions Roll 406/34.

Amen," his will begins, "the Thirde daye of September 1603 I Christopher Morley of the parishe of St Dunstones in the west London gent although sicke in bodie yet in good and perfect remembraunce." After desiring to be buried in the parish churchyard, he bequeaths to his wife Elizabeth, sole executrix, all his goods, leases, ready money, plate, jewels, bills, bonds, and other belongings, save forty shillings to each of the overseers of his will, Richard Gibson and Richard Wrench. Five witnesses attest the will, which Morley signs only by mark. It was proved by Elizabeth Morley, on October 29 following, in the court of the Commissary to the Bishop of London.[1] The fact that probate was in this court, which had jurisdiction over wills from certain parishes such as St. Dunstan's in the West, is evidence that Morley owned no goods or property in any other jurisdiction, for if he had, his will would have been proved in the Prerogative Court of Canterbury.

Of later Morleys I need mention only Christopher of Clement's Inn, who died at Reading in 1610. His will, made July 4 and proved September 18,[2] bestows money on the poor of Reading and of "Nomamly" (Normanby) in Cleveland, Yorkshire. He leaves bequests to his wife Helen, his brother James Morley, his brother-in-law Stephen "Statonstall" (Saltonstall),[3] and to Henry Morley of Reading and Henry's brother Thomas. This Christopher and others in the seventeenth century, however, were perhaps too young to have been contemporaries of Marlowe.

1. Register 1597–1603, f. 436^v.
2. Prerogative Court of Canterbury, 82 Wingfield.
3. Cf. H. F. Waters, *Genealogical Gleanings in England* (1901), II, 936.

In 1592, then, a letter addressed to "Christopher Morley, London" might have found its way to any one of at least five Christophers besides the poet: Christopher of St. Vedast's, Christopher of St. Sepulchre's, the Christophers of Clerkenwell, and Christopher of St. Dunstan's. These men must not be forgotten when we are considering to whom any particular occurrence of the name may refer. The first two, however, one a servant and the other a carpenter, would not have been described as "generosus"; nor, probably, would the Christophers of Clerkenwell, since they invariably appear in the parish registers without the ordinary prefix of respect, "Master."

Fortunately for our present purpose, we are able to specify the parish in which each one of the Christopher Morleys of London resided. None of them lived near Holywell Street, and the only one who bore the style of "gentleman" lived the farthest away, in St. Dunstan's in the West. Future research will no doubt unearth still others of the name, but it is not likely that any of them can seriously dispute the poet's claim to be the "Christopherus Marle" of the 1592 recognizance. Even without taking into consideration what we know otherwise of Marlowe's impetuous character, it is fairly to be concluded from the evidence before us that the Christopher who threatened the constable of Holywell Street was the dramatist, the only one of the name who lived in the theatrical quarter of Shoreditch.

CHAPTER VI

Norton Folgate

THE new discoveries have solved the puzzle of Marlowe's appearance at Newgate in 1589. They have brought to light an unsuspected conflict with the law in 1592, the second definite record of Marlowe's life as a playwright in London. Nor is this all: they have also at last made known to us where Marlowe lived in London, a question which seemed to be as unlikely of solution as what song the Sirens sang, or what name Achilles assumed when he hid himself among women.

The Newgate calendar of 1589 describes Marlowe as living in the same precinct with Watson, "Norton ffowlgate." Norton Folgate was not a parish but a liberty in the suburbs, outside the jurisdiction of the City of London, and consequently a good place of residence for players and others who had reason to be shy of sheriff's officers. Other liberties in and about London included the Clink, which gave shelter to the Globe, the Rose, and the Hope; the liberty of the Rolls in Chancery Lane, and the liberty of the Duchy of Lancaster outside Temple Bar, beside the somewhat similar precincts of the Blackfriars, the Whitefriars, and St. Paul's. Each liberty had its own officers of the peace, but these officers looked for their orders to the justices of Middlesex. The Lord Mayor, therefore, could take no direct action against their inhabitants.

Norton Folgate proper was a short part of the highway which led from London Bridge straight through the City as Bridge Street, Fish Street, Gracechurch Street, and Bishopsgate Street. From Bishopsgate Street Norton Folgate ran as far as Hog Lane and then became Holywell Street, leading to the church of St. Leonard's, Shoreditch. Marlowe may have lived either in the main street or in the liberty of Norton Folgate which extended on the west, south of Hog Lane, and on the east, including the site of St. Mary's Hospital, commonly called the Spital. William Rowley mentions Norton Folgate in his play *A New Wonder, A Woman Never Vext* (1632), where Bruyne, the founder of the hospital in 1197, thus announces his purpose: [1]

> Neare Norton Folgate therefore have I bought
> Ground to erect this house, which I will call
> And dedicate, *Saint Maries Hospitall.*

"In place of this Hospitall," Stow writes,[2] "and neare adioyning, are now many faire houses builded, for receipt and lodging of worshipfull persons."

That Norton Folgate shared the reputation of other London suburbs can be seen from the frequency with which it occurs in the Sessions records. For example, earlier in 1589 Simon Askewe, gentleman, was bound over to the Sessions "vpon complaint of the Constable of Norton Folgate for frequenting suspected houses in that liberty"; and in 1591 the coroner held an inquest at Norton Folgate on Thomas Bardesley, slain with a brown-bill in an affray begun against a vintner.[3] In *Father Hubburd's Tales* (1604) Middleton makes the Ant lament that he "was forcst to

1. Sig. H 1ᵛ.   2. *A Survey of London* (1908), I, 167.
3. Jeaffreson, *Middlesex County Records*, I, 186 f., 198.

retire towards the Spittle, and Shore-ditch, which as it appeared was the onely Cole-harbor and Sanctuarie for Wenches and Souldiers: where I tooke vp a poore lodging a trust, till the Sunday." [1]

The Hog Lane where Marlowe and Watson fought Bradley may now be more particularly identified. Elizabethan London had three streets of the name, all on the outskirts of the City, where the citizens had once let their hogs run free. The longest ran from Aldgate High Street to Bishopsgate. By 1626 it had already secured the name of Petticoat Lane by which it is still famous for its market, though officially rechristened Middlesex Street. Stow tells of its transformation in Elizabeth's reign: [2]

This Hogge lane stretcheth North toward Saint *Marie Spitle* without Bishopsgate, and within these fortie yeares, had on both sides fayre hedgerowes of Elme trees, with Bridges and easie stiles to passe ouer into the pleasant fieldes, very commodious for Citizens therein to walke, shoote, and otherwise to recreate and refresh their dulled spirites in the sweete and wholesome ayre, which is now within few yeares made a continuall building throughout, of Garden houses, and small Cottages: and the fields on either side be turned into Garden plottes, teynter yardes, Bowling Allyes, and such like.

Gondomar, the Spanish Ambassador to James I, had his house here. Another Hog Lane or Street, running east from Little Tower Hill, was known in 1608 as Rosemary Lane and is now Royal Mint Street.[3] The coroner's in-

---

1. Sig. E 3[v].
2. *A Survey of London* (1908), I, 127.
3. H. A. Harben, *A Dictionary of London* (1918), pp. 413, 513. A later Hog Lane is now part of Charing Cross Road, while Hammersmith has had both a Hog Lane and a Hampshire Hog Lane (Alan Stapleton, *London Lanes* [1930], pp. 112–115).

quest, however, describes the Hog Lane where Marlowe fought as in the parish of St. Giles without Cripplegate. It has been suggested to me that the street in question is Huggin Lane, between Wood Street and Gutter Lane, lying partly in Cripplegate ward. But not to mention that the only record of its being called "Hoggeslane" dates from 1234,[1] Huggin Lane is not in the parish of St. Giles but in that of St. Michael's, Wood Street. And if Bradley had been killed within the limits of London, the arrest of Marlowe and Watson would not be set down in the records of Middlesex.

The lane in which Marlowe crossed swords with Bradley can only, therefore, have been the Hog Lane which began at Norton Folgate and ran west to the windmills in Finsbury Fields. The part of Hog Lane which contained dwelling-houses lay just to the south of the Curtain theater. The map attributed to Ralph Agas (about 1570) shows a man walking in this part of Hog Lane. For the most part Hog Lane was a way through the fields, and the Agas map pictures a horse and cattle grazing on either side. On the south was the Mallow Field, twelve acres of ground extending southward to Moorfields. On the north was "the *High* field, or *Medow ground*, where the three windmills stand, commonly called *Finsbury field*," forty-five acres extending on the west to Bunhill Fields and on the east to the Earl of Rutland's lands and the highway to Holywell.[2] Both fields were, in fact, known as Finsbury Fields, because they belonged to the manor of Finsbury, a prebend of St. Paul's. They were principally used as archery

1. Harben, *A Dictionary of London*, p. 313.
2. Survey of the manor of Finsbury, 1567, printed by Strype in his edition of Stow, *A Survey of the Cities of London and Westminster* (1720), II, 101–103.

grounds for the citizens of London. On the side toward
Hog Lane each field was enclosed by a half ditch — evidently the ditch beyond which, according to the coroner's
jury, Watson could not flee without endangering his life.

The ditch even makes its appearance in an Elizabethan
play, Chapman's *Sir Giles Goosecap* (1606). Sir Giles, in-
veighing against the untrustworthy moon, tells how he followed the daylight "into *Finsburie* fieldes ith calme euen-
ing to see the winde-mils goe; & euen as I was going ouer a
ditch the moone by this light of purpose runnes me behind
a cloud, and lets me fall into the ditch by heauen." "I shall
nere loue English moone againe," the woful knight con-
cludes, "while I liue." [1]

Since Bradley was killed in the parish of St. Giles without Cripplegate, Marlowe and Watson fought him, not in
the part of Hog Lane which belonged to Norton Folgate
and Shoreditch, but in the lane between the High Field and
the Mallow Field, within Finsbury manor. [2] The present
parish of St. Giles lies within the City of London; but the
Elizabethan parish consisted of two parts, the Freedom,
within the City, and the Lordship (now in the main the
parish of St. Luke's, Old Street), in the county of Middlesex. The Lordship of Finsbury was leased by St. Paul's to
the City from 1315 to 1867, and governed by the Lord
Mayor as lord of the manor, the Recorder acting as
steward. The manor house, Finsbury Court, served as a
court-house for the Middlesex Sessions, and the Sessions
Rolls mention both Finsbury prison and pillory. [3] Accord-

---

1. III. i, sig. E 3ᵛ.

2. For the boundary between St. Leonard's and St. Giles see the maps in
Strype's edition of Stow, II, 50, 60.

3. Jeaffreson, *Middlesex County Records*, I, 64, 86; W. Denton, *Records of St.
Giles', Cripplegate* (1883), pp. 89–98.

ing to the coroner's inquest Bradley died at Finsbury, where also the jury viewed his body. His fight with Marlowe and Watson evidently took place, then, in the western part of Hog Lane, toward the windmills and Finsbury Court.

I have found at the Guildhall Library the original records of court baron for Finsbury manor, which contain references to the Theater and to Edward Alleyn and the Fortune playhouse, which Alleyn held as tenant of the manor. The volume [1] is entitled, "A Book of Records For the Mannor of Fynnesbury. 1581," but the older records copied in go back as far as 1550. Most of the entries are brief, but the only one that concerns us at present is satisfactorily full: a presentment of "the true boundes of the Manno^r of ffinsbury," set down at a manor court on October 6, 1586.[2] Finsbury manor, and therefore the parish of St. Giles, Cripplegate, within which Marlowe fought Bradley, extended eastward from Finsbury farmhouse, by a rail separating Mallow Field from Moor Field, to the common sewer that ran into Moorditch. Turning north, the boundary line took in the gardens and closes of John Worsopp, south of Hog Lane, which has derived from the Worsopp family its modern name of Worship Street. "And so," the jury declared, "the same boundes goe over the highe waye close by a barren latly builded by one Niccolles includinge the same barren and so northe as the comon sewer & waye goethe to the playe howse called the Theater And so tournethe by the same comon sewer to Dame agnes the clere," and thence westward to the new

1. Guildhall MS. 96/1.
2. Pages 25–27. An eighteenth-century copy of the bounds is in the Guildhall Record Office, Small MS. Box 29, no. 24.

houses built by Humphrey Toy, stationer, near Charter-house wall.

The dreamer in *Tarlton's News out of Purgatory* (1590), when he found a "concourse of unrulye people" at the Theater, "stept by dame Anne of Cleeres well, and went by the backside of Hogsdon." Jonson names the well in *Bartholomew Fair* (III. i), and so do Dekker in *Satiromastix* and Wilkins in *The Miseries of Enforced Marriage*, where the clown disguises it as "Demoniceaclear." [1]

The dramatists bear witness that Finsbury Fields were frequented by duelists as well as by archers. In *The Famous History of the Life and Death of Captain Thomas Stukeley* (1605) the bailiff of Finsbury, Geoffrey Blurt, says that Stukeley owes him "For fraies and bloudshed in the theater fields, Fiue marks." Stukeley's friend Jack Dudley is "in Finsbury Jaile for hurting a man behind the windmilles last Satterday." [2] The three windmills of Marlowe's day increase to six in later maps. Middleton mentions Windmill Hill in 1604,[3] while in *A Fair Quarrel* (1617, IV. i) Chaugh says, "I haue heard 'um roare from the sixe windmilles to *Islington*." Luce's father in Heywood's *The Wise Woman of Hogsdon* (1604, IV. ii) boasts that when young he had his wards and foins and quarter-blows in Tuttle and Finsbury. And in Shirley's *The Wedding* (1626, IV. i) Rawbone challenges Master Lodam, "the place *Finsbury*," and Lodam's servant Camelion frightens him with five or six windmills.

1. See E. H. Sugden, *A Topographical Dictionary to the Works of Shakespeare and his Fellow Dramatists* (1925), p. 20; and add that Richard Johnson tells the legend of Dame Annes in *The Pleasant Walks of Moorfields* (1607). The well is shown in Hole's map of the archery marks in Finsbury Fields (J. P. Malcolm, *Londinium Redivivum*, IV [1807], 26).

2. Sig. C 3ᵛ.

3. *Father Hubburd's Tales*, sig. E 3ᵛ.

Since Marlowe and Bradley met in a place so convenient for dueling, their coming together in Hog Lane may not have been entirely unpremeditated. An Elizabethan coroner's inquest generally relates only the events directly leading up to a death, without stating how the parties came to be in the place where they fought. The inquest on Bradley begins with the statement that when he and Marlowe "were fighting together in Hog Lane" Watson intervened. Since Bradley had already sought sureties of the peace against Watson and his friends, the chances are that he had either challenged or been challenged by Marlowe or Watson to settle the quarrel in the fields.

Sir Edward Sherburne told Aubrey that Ben Jonson "killed Mr. Marlow, the poet, on Bunhill, comeing from the Green-Curtain play-house." [1] The statement is commonly cited as a shining instance of Aubrey's unreliability, but Aubrey cannot fairly be blamed for setting down in good faith what his informant told him. It is easy to understand how the confusion arose in the course of eighty years. Jonson had killed a man; Marlowe had been killed; and, what made it natural for the two events to coalesce in later memory, both men had fought in the fields west of the Theater. Henslowe recorded that Gabriel Spencer, the actor, was "slayen in hogesden fylldes by the hands of bengeman Jonson, bricklayer." [2] In the indictment against Jonson the place of the quarrel is given as the fields at Shoreditch. [3] The parish register of St. Leonard's adds to the record of Spencer's burial on September 24, 1598, the words "Hogge lane," to indicate his place of residence. [4]

1. John Aubrey, 'Brief Lives,' ed. A. Clark (1898), II, 13.
2. Greg, Henslowe Papers (1907), p. 48.
3. Jeaffreson, Middlesex County Records, I, xxxviii; IV, 350.
4. J. P. Collier, Memoirs of the Principal Actors in the Plays of Shakespeare, Shakespeare Society (1846), p. xxii; verified from the register.

Not many burials from Hog Lane are to be found in the Shoreditch register, for only part of the street was included in St. Leonard's. Most of Norton Folgate, as a prebend of St. Paul's, originally belonged to the parish of St. Faith, by St. Paul's Cathedral, but in practise the people of the liberty considered it extra-parochial, and married and buried where they pleased.[1] It is consequently not easy to trace the dwellers in Norton Folgate. In 1586, a tax list shows,[2] the richest inhabitants were Thomas Fowler, Stephen Vaughan, and Nicholas Saunder, father of the younger Nicholas mentioned in the chapter on Bradley.

Hog Lane was later to be the residence of at least one actor beside Gabriel Spencer: William Beeston, son of Christopher Beeston of Shakespeare's company. When Aubrey was gathering notes for a life of Shakespeare, about 1681, he was told that the man who knew most about Shakespeare was William Beeston, "who knew all the old English poets." "He lives in Shore-ditch," Aubrey set down, "at Hoglane, within 6 dores — Norton-folgate." [3] Aubrey recorded next year that "Old Mr. Beeston, whom Mr. Dreyden calles 'the chronicle of the stage,' died at his house in Bishopsgate street without, about Bartholomew-tyde, 1682." [4]

Fortunately, Aubrey saw Beeston before he died, and learned that Shakespeare had been in his youth a school-master in the country, that he "was not a company

1. Henry Ellis, *The History and Antiquities of the Parish of Saint Leonard Shoreditch, and Liberty of Norton Folgate, in the Suburbs of London* (1798), p. 305; Kate M. Hall, "Relics of the Ancient Liberty of Norton Folgate in the Stepney Borough Museum," *The Home Counties Magazine*, V (October, 1903), 245–247.
2. Harleian MS. 366, fols. 75, 83ᵛ; Ellis, pp. 305, 326.
3. Bodleian Aubrey MS. 8, f. 45ᵛ; facsimile in E. K. Chambers, *William Shakespeare* (1930), II, 252.
4. '*Brief Lives*,' I, 97.

keeper," and that he "lived in Shoreditch." Beeston should be accurate in this part of his testimony, for Shoreditch had been the home of his family in Shakespeare's time. His father, who acted in *Every Man in his Humour* (1598), was servant to the player Augustine Phillips, who left bequests in 1605 to both Shakespeare and Christopher Beeston. Mr. Hotson has discovered that Christopher left to his son William his property in St. Leonard's, Shoreditch, and that the property included a lease of part of the Curtain estate and the freehold of the King's Head Yard, north of Hog Lane, which Christopher claimed by inheritance.[1] I can add that Thomas Middleton, the dramatist, in conveying to his brother-in-law the moiety he had inherited of the Curtain estate, names "Widowe Beston" as the late occupant of a house on the estate before 1600.[2]

Shakespeare was living before 1596 in the parish of St. Helen's, Bishopsgate, so that the period of his residence in Shoreditch probably included his earlier years in London. These were the very years when Marlowe, as the newly-found records of Middlesex Sessions now make it evident, inhabited the same theatrical quarter, in 1589 living in the liberty of Norton Folgate, and in 1592 assaulting the constables of Holywell Street in Shoreditch. In these years Shoreditch was not yet rivaled by Southwark as the region of playhouses, and the Theater and the Curtain were still the homes of the chief companies of players. James Burbage, who was a resident of Holywell Street when he built the Theater in 1576, still lived there when he was bound over by Justice Young in 1593.[3] Shakespeare, as an actor,

---

1. Hotson, *The Commonwealth and Restoration Stage* (1928), pp. 92, 98, 129, 398; C7/127/52, Sir Clement and Dame Katherine Farnham v. William Beeston.
2. Close Roll, 42 Eliz.: C 54/1693.
3. Jeaffreson, *Middlesex County Records*, I, 217.

would naturally wish to live in Shoreditch, like others of his company, and Marlowe had good reason to live near the theaters where *Tamburlaine* and *Faustus* were winning him both fame and livelihood.

Marlowe was not the only university playwright who knew Shoreditch well. Robert Greene must have been equally familiar with the district, for his bastard son, Fortunatus Greene, was buried at St. Leonard's on August 12, 1593.[1] "Halliwell," added in the register, shows that the child's mother, Greene's mistress, lived not far from the Theater. She was the sister of Cutting Ball, as Gabriel Harvey relates in the second of his *Foure Letters*, dated from London September 5, 1592, the day after the burial of Greene:[2]

his imployinge of Ball, (surnamed, cutting Ball) till he was intercepted at Tiborne, to leauy a crew of his trustiest companions, to guarde him in daunger of Arrestes: his keping of the foresaid Balls sister, a sorry ragged queane, of whome hee had his base sonne, *Infortunatus Greene*.

The mother of Fortunatus was the sole companion of Greene's last illness, save his hostess and Mistress Appleby; and Harvey writes of Greene's "buriall yesterday in the New-churchyard neere Bedlam."[3] Bedlam stood just outside Bishopsgate north of St. Botolph's church, on the way to Norton Folgate and Shoreditch. Harvey does not specify where Greene died, but he names Shoreditch as one of the poet's haunts, together with the Bankside and Southwark. *Greenes Groats-Worth of Witte* (1592) con-

1. Collier, *Memoirs of the Principal Actors*, p. xx; parish register.
2. *Foure Letters, and certaine Sonnets: Especially touching Robert Greene, and other parties, by him abused*, sig. B 2ᵛ.
3. Sig. B 3ᵛ.

firms by a punning allusion Harvey's statement that Cutting Ball was hanged. The book speaks of the shameful end of some among Greene's companions, "of which one, brother to a Brothell hee kept, was trust vnder a tree as round as a Ball." [1]

No one seems to have noticed that some light may be thrown on the mother of Greene's son Fortunatus by the story of the last days of Richard Tarlton, the greatest of pre-Shakespearian actors. On his deathbed in 1588 Tarlton wrote a letter beseeching the aid of Sir Francis Walsingham against "a sly fellow on(e) Addames being more fuller of law then vertew," who would try to get his estate away from Tarlton's mother and his son, "a sillie old widdow of forscore years of age and a pore infant of the age of six yeares." The boy Philip, Tarlton reminded Walsingham, was the godson of Sir Philip Sidney and bore his name. In behalf of herself and Philip, "Katheryne Tarlton wyddowe mother of Richarde Tarlton deceased" brought a Chancery bill against Robert Adams on October 23, 1588, signed by her counsel Francis Beaumont (the dramatist's father) and Thomas Lancaster. Adams in his answer claimed to have been sent for by Tarlton in his last illness, "he lyenge at that tyme in the howse of one Em Ball in Shordiche in the Cowntye of Midd*lesex* as this Defendant taketh it she beinge a woman of verye bad reputac*i*on." [2] The parish register of St. Leonard's, Shoreditch, shows that the house where Tarlton died was in "Haliwelstret." [3] Several persons named Ball appear in the register, but most of them

1. Sig. E 2.
2. C 3/229/121; printed (in ten copies only) by J. O. Halliwell, *Papers Respecting Disputes which Arose from Incidents at the Death-Bed of Richard Tarlton, the Actor, in the Year 1588* (1866).
3. Collier, *Memoirs of the Principal Actors*, p. 15; parish register.

belonged to the family of John Ball in the "parsonage" or Church End, possibly the John Ball, gardener, who in 1586 claimed the parish clerk's house as concealed chantry lands.[1] His wife Alice was buried on November 5, 1588, and an Awdry Ball on March 24, 1592/3, both from the parsonage. Among others of the name were "Haile Ball," daughter of John, christened January 31, 1573/4, from Loveday's tenements, and Deborah Ball, daughter of Nicholas, buried in 1580 from "Allens" — the rents of Giles Allen, landlord of the Theater. Greene's mistress, the sister of Cutting Ball, if not herself Em Ball, was in all likelihood her daughter or otherwise closely related.

Possibly Greene was staying in Holywell, where his mistress lived, at the same time that Marlowe was bound over to keep the peace toward the constables of Holywell Street in May, 1592. Greene was charged with continually shifting his lodgings,[2] and Marlowe, for all we know, may have done the same. Our only certain knowledge of Marlowe's residence is that he was of Norton Folgate at the time of his arrest in 1589. In 1592 he may still have lived in Norton Folgate or he may have taken lodgings in the precinct of Holywell in order to be even closer to the playhouses. It was at the Theater and the Curtain, of course, that most of his plays first came upon the stage. In *The Black Book* (1604) Middleton makes Lucifer allude to "one of my *Diuells* in Docter *Faustus*, when the olde Theater crackt and frighted the Audience."[3]

Marlowe, Greene, and Shakespeare — such men once walked the streets of the straggling suburb beyond Bish-

1. Ellis, *The History of Shoreditch*, pp. 299–301.
2. Harvey, *Foure Letters*, sig. B 2ᵛ; *Greenes Groats-Worth of Witte*, sig. E 2.
3. Sig. B 4.

opsgate. Unluckily for Marlowe, Shoreditch was full of worse companions than playwrights or actors. One of them was Robert Poley, the spy who witnessed the death of Marlowe in the tavern at Deptford. The State Papers contain a reference to Robert Poley of Shoreditch as a Government intelligencer in 1591, and a letter written from Hogsdon in 1597, signed "Ro. P." in Poley's hand.[1] I find in the probate acts of the Archdeaconry of London that administration on the goods of Rose Crayford, widow, of Shoreditch, having been renounced by the vicar of St. Leonard's, Mr. Edward Vaughan, was granted on November 23, 1593, to Robert "Polye," the other supervisor named in her nuncupative will.[2] Shoreditch, therefore, seems to have been Poley's quarter of London as well as that of Shakespeare and the Burbages.

1. S. P. Dom. Eliz. 238/140, 262/58.
2. Archdeaconry of London, Act Book 2, fols. 132^v, 134.

CHAPTER VII

Douai

THE primary authority for the life of any author is what he tells us in his own works, and it seems hardly too much to expect of a biographer that, if he looks anywhere at all for material (other than in the accounts of his predecessors), he should look here. This first step is by no means always taken. Even in the comparatively brief compass of the published writings of Watson, anyone who has the curiosity to begin reading them through will make a discovery on the very first page. Watson's dedicatory verses to his Latin translation of the *Antigone* contain an important passage of autobiography. The verses are actually published by Arber, but evidently in the swift, efficient manner of the business man whose letters are admittedly "Dictated, but not read." To be sure, the lines are in Latin, and that language has proved as successful in concealing their contents, not only from Arber but also from later biographers, as cipher could have been. Concealment, however, was no part of Watson's intention. He wrote in Latin in order that the widest possible audience might hear him; and he would have been surprised to learn that it was only from *Meliboeus*, which he wisely translated into English, that scholars three centuries later were to gather that he had been abroad at all. They quote what he says of his sojourn in Paris (from the English version); but they give no hint of his having traveled in Italy as well as in France, nor of the unusual length of his residence on the Continent. Professor Moore Smith [1] has called attention to the information furnished by the verses in question, but Sir Edmund Chambers [2] remains unaware of it in his discussion of Watson. Yet Watson's experience of foreign countries is a matter of some interest in accounting for the unusual breadth of his reading in Italian, French, and neo-Latin poetry, for the form his own poetry took, and for his high reputation and consequent influence upon his contemporaries in England.

Watson made his first appearance as an author by turning the *Antigone* from Greek into Latin. On July 31, 1581, John Wolfe paid his sixpence for the license of "Aphoclis Antigone," [3] entered, as Francis Turner Palgrave put it, "by a clerk of Dogberry's order." [4] The printed volume has the title correctly: "Sophoclis Antigone. Jnterprete Thoma Watsono J. V. studioso." To the translation Watson adds Latin poems of his own, suggested by the play: *Pompae*, which recall the emblem-writers or Spenser's *Visions*; and *Themata*, which he describes on the title-page as "sententiis refertissima." As patron for the volume he chose Philip Howard, Earl of Arundel and Surrey, and grandson of the poet Surrey.

The Latin text of the dedication is accessible in Arber's edition of Watson. Since it does not seem to have been

1. *Notes and Queries*, 12th series, VII (1920), 422–423.
2. *The Elizabethan Stage*, III, 506.
3. Edward Arber, *A Transcript of the Registers of the Company of Stationers of London*, II (1875), 398.
4. F. T. Palgrave, *North American Review*, CXIV (1872), 90.

often read in our time, for the sake of convenience I supply a translation:

To the most noble peer, illustrious by many titles, *Philip Howard*, Earl of Arundel, *Thomas Watson* wishes entire felicity.

Receive, O Earl richly endowed with noble ancestors and made richer in nobility by virtues and by the gifts of the Muses, the youthful verse of even so humble a poet, and glance over this slight result of great labor. Not mine is the Muse of Callimachus, or of Philetos of Cos; and the fox has nothing to offer but his pelt. But the gods look to the minds of men, not to their gifts; therefore do you, the equal of those above, imitate the gods. What if this little book of mine be full of errors? what if there is fault to be found with my indifferent verse? Cynthia surveys both the shining and the dark with her countenance; Phoebus visits both shining and dark with his rays; and may your graciousness receive with your accustomed countenance such things as are either shining or dark in my verse. Apollo demands the songs of Marsyas, Minerva desires Arachne's web, Croesus takes pleasure in the gift of Irus; Apollo, though the god of music, does not disdain songs, or Minerva, though bountiful, a web, or Croesus, though powerful, a gift. And you possess lesser verses than mine (if report says true) in the form of a gift.

Indeed, I do not hold the poets of old in so great account that I should wish there to be nothing in our own praise. It may be I have written with the good will of both Phoebus and Minerva, whence the offspring of my striving may receive a triumph. If you judge it well, happy in having you for judge I shall put spurs to my powers, and gladly do what many have often asked, so that many writings shall rustle under the weight of the press.

Let Momus himself murmur empty words beneath his breath, and envious Zoilus mark it with his pitchy claw, the verdict of your judgment will prevail over both, and place on my brow the wreath of laurel. Then shall I be called happy enough to be your poet, and to become, with Ganymede, the attendant of Jove. Indeed, long ago I began to hope for this advantage, while I altogether devoted my early years to study, and while, far from my native land, I passed a lustrum and a half, learning to utter words of diverse sounds.[1]

A lustrum and a half carries the beginning of his travels at least as far back as 1573 or 1574. It is surprising to learn that he had thus spent a whole term of apprenticeship abroad; he would appear almost a stranger in England. His familiarity with Italy explains very well, however, why his work had the effect of novelty to the English, whose poetry had absorbed Italian influences since Wyatt and Surrey, but had so mixed them into the native stream that Watson's elaborately regular style must have seemed purely Italian and Petrarchan, and therefore admirable and to be imitated.

Watson continues the story of his education abroad:[2]

At that time I was taking careful note of the tongues and manners of Italy, and of your language and manners, learned France. So far as I was able, I paid worship to the Muses, wherever I went. Justinian, too, was especially dear. But Mars often broke in upon reluctant Pallas, wars were often obstacles to my study. Yet I fled from camps, save those of Apollo which sheltered the Muses and the devout Graces. Bartolus, you were large, and it was not permitted to carry about your legal knots, nor yours, ingenious Baldus.

1. "Dumque procul patria lustrum mediumque peregi,
    Discere, diuersis œdere verba sonis."

2. "Tum satis Italiæ linguas moresque notabam;
    Et linguam, et mores Gallia docta tuos.
  Vt potui, colui Musas, quocunque ferebar:
    Charus et imprimis Justinianus erat.
  Saepe sed inuitam turbauit Pallada Mauors,
    Saepe meo studio bella fuere moræ.
  Castra tamen fugi, nisi quæ Phœbeia castra
    Cum Musis Charites continuere pias.
  Bartole magnus eras, neque circumferre licebat,
    Nec legum nodos Balde diserte tuos; . . ."

When he finished his translation of Sophocles, Watson says, he wished to tear it up or cast it in the fire, because the Greek was so much better. But a crowd of good judges, *prudentum turba virorum*, overruled him, and praised him in a chorus of eulogies. He revised his work, therefore, and began to look for a patron, "one who should be a dear foster-child of Apollo and the Muses, and love the waters of Helicon." He has found the very man, so he hopes, in Arundel, whom he reminds that even the mouse was once of use to the lion, and to whom he wishes, finally, as many happy years as the deer lives.

Philip Howard, godson of the King of Spain and himself of a dark and drawn Spanish countenance, would have been Duke of Norfolk but for his father's hope of marriage with Mary Stuart. He had been married at the age of twelve to a devout Catholic, and his first tutor had been Gregory Martin, later translator of the Rheims Testament, but he himself was in 1581 known only as an extravagant young courtier with no reputation whatever for either religion or morals. At the time when he failed so signally in his attempt to seduce Gabriel Harvey's sister Mercy,[1] men would have been astonished to hear that he would some day be beatified. He became "Venerable" in 1886, and the process for his beatification is now going on at Rome.

Arundel's biographers have not known of Watson's dedication to him. They name only three books dedicated to him in his pre-Catholic period: two works by William Temple in defense of Ramus against the Catholic Everard Digby, and a work by James Bell against Bishop Osorius,

1. G. C. Moore Smith, *Notes and Queries*, 11th series, III (1911), 261; E. J. L. Scott, *Letter-Book of Gabriel Harvey, A. D. 1573–1580*, Camden Society (1884), pp. 143–158; Virginia Woolf, *The Common Reader, Second Series* (1932), pp. 11–15.

both strongly Protestant books.[1] Watson's choice of Arundel as a patron, therefore, carries no suggestion of Catholic sympathies, any more than his dedication the following year to the Earl of Oxford, who, according to the French ambassador, Mauvissière, had become a secret Catholic about 1576 but at Christmas in 1580 denounced Lord Henry Howard and his other Catholic friends to the Queen.[2]

The description Watson gives of his studies on the Continent is interesting for his statement that he was especially devoting himself to Roman law (Justinian). In all the Latin works which Watson published he calls himself "Thomas Watsonus I. V. studiosus," student in either law ("Iuris Vtriusque"). The critics and biographers of Watson have not understood this phrase. Most of them seem to have had a vague idea that he was a student at one of the Inns of Court, turning over, like Donne's friend, "Th'immense great volumes of the common law." But "either law" refers, of course, to the canon and the civil law, and has no reference to the study of the common law of England. Watson's own allusions to the authorities he studied are not to Littleton, Bracton, or Fitzherbert, but to Justinian, Bartolus, and Baldus.

Bartolus of Sassoferrato, the most famous master of the dialectical school of jurists, wrote a commentary on the Code of Justinian which was held to rival the original in authority and had in Spain the force of law. In the sixteenth century Dumoulin called him "le premier et le

1. *The Ven. Philip Howard, Earl of Arundel, 1557-1595*, Catholic Record Society, XXI (1919), 26.

2. The same, pp. 29-30; B. M. Ward, *The Seventeenth Earl of Oxford* (1928), pp. 29-30.

coryphée des interprètes en droit." Watson could have read his works either in the ten folio volumes published at Lyons in 1544, in the edition published at Turin in 1577, or in single volumes.[1] As an exercise in ingenuity Bartolus also wrote a *Processus Satanæ contra Virginem, coram judice Jesu,* in which the Devil claims Man by long possession, but fails to make good his title against the defendant. He died in 1357 at Perugia, where his magnificent monument bears only two words, "Ossa Bartoli." His pupil Baldus de Ubaldis became doctor of civil law in 1344 at the age of seventeen, and later professor at Bologna, Perugia, Pisa, Florence, Padua, and Pavia. He achieved his great reputation as a jurisconsult less through his writings than through his activity in public affairs and the consultations in which he assisted Urban VI against Clement.[2]

Watson had probably carried on his study of the Roman law in Italy, where the most famous schools in his time were at Padua and Bologna. Tasso, a dozen years earlier, had been one of the first to study in the splendid new buildings which Bologna had erected at the instance of St. Charles Borromeo and his uncle the Pope — Bologna, not only the mother of all modern universities, but the first to revive, under Gratian and Irnesius respectively, the study of both the canon and the civil law. Padua, however, backed by the wealth of Venice, now ranked first

1. Harvey quotes Bartolus apropos of Greene in *Foure Letters, and certaine Sonnets,* sig. F 1: "A Gibeline may haue a Guelph to his sonne, as Barthol saith."

2. F. C. von Savigny, *Geschichte des Römischen Rechts im Mittelalter,* VI, chapters 53, 55; C. N. S. Woolf, *Bartolo of Sassoferrato* (1914). Two works of Bartolus have been translated into English: *Bartolus on the Conflict of Laws,* by J. H. Beale (Cambridge, Mass., 1914), and *De Tyrannia,* by Ephraim Emerton, in *Human Tyranny* (Cambridge, Mass., 1925).

among European universities. More foreigners came to
it than to any of its rivals, not only because of the emi-
nence of its professors, but also because it was the university town of Venice, the irresistible magnet that drew
all travelers. Sidney and Lodowick Bryskett were here
in 1573/4, and a remarkable series of English poets visited
Padua during the next century. There were English and
Scottish "Nations" at the university until 1738. The
principal other Italian universities at which Watson
might have studied were Siena and Ferrara, Pavia and
Turin, and Perugia, whose law school Bartolus and Baldus
had made the equal of Bologna's, and from which Alberi-
cus Gentilis fled for religion to Oxford to publish in 1588
his *De Jure Belli* and thus to lay the foundations of inter-
national law.

Watson's reference to the wars which interrupted his
education applies especially to France. Italy was now
fairly quiet under the overlordship of Spain and of the
Medici; but in France this was the time of the civil wars
and of the formation of the League in 1576. What he
says of avoiding camps and sticking to his studies recalls
the famous answer of Jacques Cujas, when pressed about
this same time to take sides in the civil wars: *Nihil hoc
ad edictum praetoris*, "this has nothing to do with Roman
law," of which he was a more brilliant interpreter than
even Bartolus. If Watson was a serious student of the
municipal law, he would certainly have sought to study
under Cujas, its foremost Renaissance master, as did
De Thou and Joseph Scaliger, whom the great civilian
saved from the massacre of St. Bartholomew. So renowned
was Cujas even in his own age that in Germany scholars
were taught to raise their hats at the mention of his name,

and he had to refuse a constant flow of offers, from Gregory XIII, from Angers and Toulouse, from Besançon and Avignon. Watson would have found him teaching at Valence in Savoy until June, 1575, then at Bourges, until in November the religious wars drove him for a year or more to Paris, where the King welcomed him and the Pope gave him special permission to teach, despite Honorius III's prohibition of the study of civil law at Paris. Watson may at least have heard Cujas lecture here; but probably he gave much more of his thought to the Muses than to Justinian. If he had gone deeper, he would perhaps not have cited Bartolus and Baldus alone, without mentioning the great humanist who had introduced into law the historical method and the study of original manuscripts. But it would be enough for him that the Italian names ran more smoothly in Latin verse than the name Cujacius. He shows more familiarity with the work of Stephanus Forcatulus, whom he follows and cites in his 68th Passion, and who in 1554 had been chosen to the professorship of civil law at Toulouse, when only twenty years of age, instead of the much more learned Cujas. Forcatel was both lyric poet and civilian. In this he resembled Cino of Pistoia, the friend of Dante and professor at Siena, Perugia, and Florence, where he was the master of Petrarch as well as of Bartolus. Watson, who had the same double ambition, would be pleased, though sober lawyers have frowned, at the imaginative titles Forcatel gave his legal works, *Aviarium Juris Civilis* and *Cupido Jurisperitus*.

Whatever cities Watson visited during his seven or eight years in Italy and France, he no doubt went like other travelers to Venice, possibly to Rome, certainly to Paris.

We are not reduced entirely to conjecture, for I have been fortunate enough to find definite record of a part of his journeying. Only a few European universities, such as Leyden, have published their admission registers for this period. The diary of the English College at Douai, however, yields the following entry under October, 1576: "15 die D. Watsonus Parisios hinc abiit." In the absence of a Christian name such a record too often only tantalizes us with a possible but doubtful identity. Fortunately, another entry in May, 1577, makes the matter clearer: "15 die Mr Tho. Watsonus e Parisiis huc revertitur et post aliquot dies ad nostra communia est admissus." There were other Watsons abroad at this time,[1] but there is no trace of any Thomas Watson except the poet. Since he himself tells us that he was studying law and in his Latin works regularly signs himself "Iuris Vtriusque studiosus," it is satisfactory to find him thus described on his next appearance in the diary: "Circa hoc tempus exierunt e communibus nostris Mr Burnus, Watsonus, Harleus, et alii juris studiosi." This memorandum follows the diarist's entry for July 10, 1577. In August Watson bade Douai goodbye: "Die 7 occasione turbarum ingruentium discesserunt in Angliam Mr Watsonus, Mr Robinsonus, Mr Griffettus et alii nonnulli."[2] The last three records clearly refer to the same person. Of the first I have felt some doubt, since the "D." for "Dominus" would ordinarily imply that the Watson in question had his B. A. degree, for which the poet in 1576 seems rather young, though it is true that he was precocious. But the

1. *Calendar of State Papers, Foreign Series, of the Reign of Elizabeth, 1575–77* (1880), p. 567; *1579–1580*, pp. 219, 251.

2. T. F. Knox, *The First and Second Diaries of the English College, Douay* (1878), pp. 112, 121, 125, 127.

diarist is not always consistent in these details, and since the Thomas Watson of the second entry had been at Douai before, and meanwhile at Paris, like the first Watson, they are presumably the same. No other Watson appears in the diary until the arrival in 1580/81 at Rheims, not at Douai, of the William Watson, "puer," who in 1603 was to imagine himself as Lord Chancellor and to lose his life in the Bye Plot for which Raleigh went to the Tower.

Marlowe, we remember, was suspected in 1587 of being "determined to have gone beyond the seas to Reames and there to remaine." [1] The danger of this suspicion was that to any Englishman of his time Rheims meant first of all the seminary of the English Catholic exiles. The seminary was the same institution which had begun as the English College of the University of Douai. The followers of the Prince of Orange drove its teachers and students from Flanders to seek a temporary refuge in Rheims from 1578 to 1593. In view of the rumor of Marlowe's purpose, it is worth while to form in our minds a picture of what the institution was like. The college at Douai and Rheims has a particular interest, too, as the first of all English colleges established outside England. Whether or not Marlowe ever visited it at Rheims, he had in all probability heard life in the college at Douai fully described, from personal experience, by his friend Watson.

Scholars in the past have not been well acquainted with the sources for the Elizabethan history of the Catholics, and they have used too rarely such admirably edited series as *Records of the English Catholics under the Penal Laws*

---

1. *Acts of the Privy Council*, XV (1897), 141; Hotson, *The Death of Christopher Marlowe*, p. 58.

or the *Publications of the Catholic Record Society.* Mr.
H. S. Bennett in his recent edition of *The Massacre at
Paris*[1] ascribes the founding of the English College at
Douai to "William Parsons," a mythical person made
like the Centaur out of two — Dr. William Allen and
Dr. Robert Parsons. Dr. Boas tells us that the college
was founded by the Pope at his own expense.[2] He is here
misled by the Cardinal of Como,[3] but the facts are easily
accessible in the *Douay Diaries* or in the *Dictionary of
National Biography.* Pius V gave his blessing after the
college had been founded in 1568, but it was Gregory XII
who in 1575 assigned it an annual pension of a hundred gold
crowns. The credit for founding the college and for making
it so immediate and so striking a success belongs to Dr.
William Allen, later Cardinal Allen.[4] On a pilgrimage
to Rome he had conversed with Dr. Vendeville, professor
of canon law at Douai, who was hoping to carry out a
project for the conversion of the infidels or for the rescue
of Christian slaves out of Barbary. When his plans fell
through, Allen fired him with enthusiasm for establishing
an educational center about which the exiled or suppressed
English Catholics might rally. Vendeville suggested that
the students be trained as missionaries to England, and
it was he who secured the money to establish the seminary
as the first college in his own university, Douai. The
university had been opened by Philip of Spain in 1561
to combat the growing Protestantism of the Flemings.
Louvain furnished its staff of professors, but its first

1. 1931, p. 241.
2. *Marlowe and his Circle*, p. 23.
3. *Calendar of State Papers, Rome,* II (1926), 435.
4. Knox, *Diaries,* and *Letters and Memorials of William, Cardinal Allen*
(1882); Martin Haile, *An Elizabethan Cardinal, William Allen* (1914).

Chancellor was Dr. Richard Smith, late regius professor of divinity at Oxford. The college opened on Michaelmas Day, 1568. Allen's right hand, and his first prefect of studies, was Richard Bristow, who had entertained Queen Elizabeth brilliantly with his oratory at Oxford, and who with Allen revised what was to become the Douai Bible. Edward Campion and Cuthbert Mayne came as students. Several former Oxford fellows joined the group, including the authors Thomas Stapleton, who translated Bede and wrote a life of Sir Thomas More in *Tres Thomæ*, and Richard White, whose favorite study was English history and who edited eleven books of *Historiæ Britanniæ*, beside offering an explanation of St. Ursula and the eleven thousand virgins. If Watson pursued his legal studies at Douai, he probably attended the lectures of Vitus (the Latin name of White), who was regius professor of civil and canon law in the university, doctor in both laws from Padua, head of the *Societas juris peritorum*, Marchiennes College, and who was chosen by the Pope as rector of the university and *Comes Palatinus*.

No better description could be given of the college and of the different kinds of people who came to it than that which Dr. Allen sent to his chief ally, Vendeville, in 1578 or 1580.[1] "We began more diligently," he writes of the years just preceding,

to animate our people to the work, to procure alms from our country, to summon the choicest wits from the universities (though many of all ranks were flocking to us of their own accord). . . . The rest who came, gentlemen's sons, who were studying humanities, philosophy or jurisprudence, and who either of their own accord or through the exhortations of catho-

---

1. Knox, *Diaries*, pp. xxxiv f. (cf. p. xxiv), and Haile, p. 145.

lic relations and friends had been moved by the fame of the seminary to seek here a catholic education, were kept by us in the college for a time, but at their own not the common charge, until according to their age and condition they had been duly catechised and reconciled to the church by penance for their previous life and schism. There came at the same time not a few who were simply heretics, and even heretical ministers and preachers, all of whom being moved to penance through our instructions and conversation were not only sincerely reconciled to the church, but after a year or two spent under the college discipline desired to become priests. . . . Besides these, all who came to Douay on business with the English students (and many came for many reasons; and travellers too on their road to France, Italy or Brabant often turned aside to see their friends or the seminary about which there was already much talk), all these men, who were for the most part devoid of all religion or at least schismatics [Catholics who attended Protestant services], were pressed to remain a few days with us; and many consented to do so. And if they were poor, we caused them to be kept at the common expense for thirty days, until they knew the chief heads of the catholic religion, had learned to confess their sins properly, and were reconciled to God. Thus we acted towards many persons with great fruit; and they returning home glorified God for the things which they had seen, and persuaded many others to leave all and come to us at Douay, or at least to come once to hear and see us, as some heretics had done.

Allen's letter makes it evident that Watson could have visited the college without necessarily being a Catholic. He may have been one, and in any case a boy who had spent so many years in France and Italy would tend to be assimilated to the prevailing religion. Allen, however, admits that curiosity was the motive which brought many of the temporary visitors: the desire to see for themselves this little band of learned men who by training boys es-caped from England were hoping to bring about the overthrow of Elizabeth and her whole system of political and ecclesiastical government.

Watson's first patron, the Earl of Arundel, had for his private tutor Gregory Martin, author of the English translation of the Bible which was revised by Allen and Bristow and published at Rheims and at Douai as the standard Catholic version. Writing in 1575 to Edmund Campion, then at Prague, Martin tells of "the swarms of theological students and candidates for holy orders who were daily coming or rather flying to the college at the mere report of such magnificent liberality" as the Pope's pension of a hundred crowns. He thus describes the college where both he and Campion had been students:[1]

It was a beautiful sight which I beheld when I was lately there. In that refectory where in our time we sat down about six at one table, nearly sixty men and youths of the greatest promise were seated at three tables eating so pleasantly a little broth, thickened merely with the commonest roots, that you could have sworn they were feasting on stewed raisins and prunes, English delicacies.

The frugality of the college was such that several of its first members, including the former Dean of Christ Church, Oxford, John Marshall, could not stand the fare, and since fasting twice a week was also required, it is not surprising that Watson and other law students withdrew from the commons before they withdrew from Douai. The Harley of this entry, like Watson, returned to England in August, 1577, and when a "Harleus" next appears in the diary, in December, 1580, he is called "Oxoniensis."

The movements of Watson recorded in the diary are a barometer of the political changes that made life in Douai

1. Knox, *Diaries*, p. xxxvi, 310.

more or less dangerous. At Michaelmas, 1576, the college held one hundred and twenty students; by New Year's, only forty-two remained. "D. Watsonus" left for Paris on October 15. Allen himself, persuaded by his friends that his life was not safe in Douai, withdrew to Paris on November 8, and a month later Stapleton, White, and Martin set out for Rome. By spring, however, Don John had the upper hand in Flanders, and the English flowed back to Douai. There was much popular feeling against them as pensioners of the hated King of Spain. In June Bristow warned the scholars to walk less frequently in the streets. After Don John was forced to withdraw to Namur, the danger reached its height. "Now," records the diary for August 6, 1577, "the old perils from the populace began as it were to kindle anew, and very great fear once more overwhelmed us." The crowd in the streets called after Dr. Ely, "Traitor!" That very morning several townsmen asked members of the college, "Were not all the Englishmen's throats cut (*jugulati*) last night?" seeming surprised to see them still walking about. The Spanish governor assured the English that this was but "an ill-advised rumor of the mob," but we can now understand why, "because of the disturbances coming on," "Mr Watsonus . . . et alii nonnulli" left the next day for England. Even the voyage across the Channel was not without risk, for a few weeks earlier new arrivals at Douai told how Godsalf and Scott, sailing for England on a French vessel, fell in with "Anglos pyratas" and only with great danger escaped with their lives.[1]

The Prince of Orange's governor took command of the town the following February, and on March 22, 1577/8,

1. Knox, *Diaries*, pp. 124, 127.

ordered the English to leave Douai. They had in consequence to exchange the protection of the Spanish King for that of the French, finding refuge at Rheims. Douai invited them back in November, and Don John offered to seat them at Louvain, but the university there was now a desert, with horses stabled in the ruined colleges. At Rheims they remained until 1593, for, though the townspeople hated them because they were English, the Duke of Guise and his brother the Cardinal favored them. Hence Marlowe made King Henry recount Guise's protection of the seminarists as one of the crimes which justified his assassination:

> Did he not draw a sorte of English priestes
> From Doway to the Seminary at Remes
> To hatch forth treason gainst their naturall Queene? [1]

These lines are more patriotic than dramatically appropriate, for in the eyes of Henry III it was hardly a crime to advance the cause of his religion in England. But they show very well how to the ordinary Englishman, for whom Marlowe was writing, the seminarists of Douai and Rheims seemed an ever-threatening danger second only to that of invasion by the Armada.

---

1. *The Massacre at Paris*, quoted by A. K. Gray, *P. M. L. A.*, XLIII (1928), 686.

CHAPTER VIII

The Wise Man of St. Helen's

IF WATSON returned to England in August, 1577, there is no trace of him for the next two years. At this time he was probably composing such early works as he mentions in 1582: *De Remedio Amoris*, "whiche he wrote long since," and his Latin verses "made long agoe vpon the loue abuses of *Iuppiter* in a certaine peece of worke written in the commendation of women kinde." [1] His biographers have known nothing of him before the publication of the *Antigone* in 1581. Among the Lansdowne Manuscripts at the British Museum, however, Mr. Hotson has found an examination in which Thomas Watson testifies that about 1579 he was lodging in Westminster. It is a pleasure to acknowledge Mr. Hotson's generosity in giving me the reference to this interesting document: Lansdowne MS. 53, no. 79 (folios 162 and 163).

The importance of the Lansdowne Manuscripts is, of course, that they preserve a large section of the correspondence of Lord Burghley, the part which was in charge of his secretary Michael Hicks. The paper in question occurs among "Examinations taken by m^r Dalton, touching one m^{ris} Burnell, y^t gave out her self K. Philips daughter." Dalton took the examinations by order from the Privy Council, and what he learned from witnesses on

1. Notes to Passions 1 and 75 in *The* Ἑκατομπαθία.

August 8, 1587, led to the summoning of Watson and the following examination, which I quote in full:

Thomas Watson late of Sᵗ Ellenes in London gen*tleman* examined the xijᵗʰ daye of August 1587: beinge demaunded wheather he knoweth a gentlewoman called Mʳˢ Burnell sayeth that he doth knowe her very well & sayth that the first acquaint-aunce he had with her was at westm*inster* aboute viij yeares past in a howse of one Walle⟨r⟩ wheare she & her husbande did lye & wheare also he himselfe did nowe & then l⟨ye⟩ wᵗh one Mʳ Beale a preacher & his acquaintaunce in Oxforde before: at ⟨which⟩ time he remembreth she had talke of an old woman that dwelte in the Contrye that had toulde that she was better borne then she was taken or to like effecte to wᶜʰ speach he sayeth he said nothinge & is very sure that neither she in his heareinge nor him selfe did ever saye that she was or that it might be she was kinge phillip or quene Maryes childe, or that it might be she was the Childe of the one or of thother, neyther eu*er* did saye that she had some mark*es* vpon her bodye that heareafter shoulde appeare [after] greater, neither ever hearde her saye that she had the mark*es* of Englande on her bodye neither ever hearde any p*er*son so saye./

It is a curious story that the other examinants have to tell. "John Warner of Strondegrene in the County of Middlesex gen*tleman*" relates that on Friday last in the morning Edward Burnell, gentleman, came to speak with him and desired his counsel and advice, "alledgeinge that his wife heareinge that Sʳ ffraunc*is* drake had brought the shipp called the Phillip of Spayne: said his Mʳ meane-ing the kinge of Spayne would not be longe after & farther that she was the daughter of king Phillip & it mighte be Queene Mary was her mother & yᵗ she had yᵉ Armes of England on her bodye." Drake had returned to Plymouth in June, bringing in the great carack *San Felipe* with its spices and silks and jewels; and the burning question in

England was whether, after this brilliant thrust at the King of Spain, the Armada would now sail this year, as had been expected, or the next. The remarkable testimony of Warner was corroborated in every point by his wife Avis.

Dalton now examined, kindly but thoroughly, Anne Burnell herself, whom he was keeping in his house in order to judge her behavior and state of mind. From his report we can imagine her, a quiet and modest gentlewoman, but with eyes brooding and a little wild, answering slowly the questions he put:

first toucheing the wordes that the king of Spayne would not be longe after she vtterly denieth the speach of them but she confesseth that she said she was king Phillips Childe as she hath bin toulde but denieth that euer she said Quene Mary was her mother . . . sayeing that she thancked god she never had so litle witt as to thincke it possible.

She acknowledged having said that she had the arms of England on her body.

"Who was it," asked Dalton, "that first put it into your head that you were King Philip's child?" To this she replied,

that she beinge at wingborne in the Countye of Notingham about viij yeares past wᵗʰ Mʳˢ Burnell her mother in lawe had talke wᵗʰ one commonly called the witch of Norrall who tould her that she was a spaniardes birde & that she had markes aboute her wᶜʰ would more appeare herafter & that she did not knowe her owne father for it was a wise childe that did so & was very importunate to haue somewhat of her & therevpon she gaue the said witch a bande that was aboute her necke & a bracelett of amber from her arme.

The witch's parish was Norwell, north of Newark and Southwell, and four or five niles from Winkbourn, on the

Winkle. William Burnell, Auditor to Henry VIII, had bought in 1548 the manor of Winkbourn, formerly belonging to the Knights of St. John of Jerusalem, and conveyed it in 1570 to his son William, who received seventy-eight pounds a year for the springs there (mineral springs still in use) when the Countess of Rutland lived at Winkbourn Hall after the Earl's death in 1588.[1] Edward Burnell was the second son. His own mother, Constance Blundeville, had died in St. Botolph Aldersgate in 1562, and his father had married the next year Ellen Goche, widow,[2] who was evidently the "mother-in-law," now once more a widow, whom they were visiting. She had been a co-executor with William Burnell to her earlier husband, Robert Goche of Chilwell, Notts, whose will[3] I shall quote elsewhere for the interesting plans he makes for his son and heir Barnaby Goche or Googe, the poet of *Eglogs, Epytaphes, and Sonettes* (1563). Ellen Burnell, therefore, was step-mother to Barnaby Googe as well as to Edward Burnell.

At Michaelmas following, Anne went on,

she came to London & did lye at westm*inster* & happened there to be in Company of a gent*leman* that was said to be very well learned & he fallinge in talke wth her said she was proude but if she knewe her selfe she would be the proudest woman in the p*a*rishe whearevpon she calling to minde what the witch of Norrall had said to her tould him that it was tould her by an

1. *Thoroton's History of Nottinghamshire* (1797), III, 128; *The Visitations of the County of Nottingham* (Harleian Society, 1871), p. 99; Historical MSS. Commission, *The MSS. . . . at Belvoir Castle*, I (1888), 124; IV (1905), 402; Cornelius Brown, *A History of Nottinghamshire* (1891), p. 152.

2. *Allegations for Marriage Licences Issued by the Bishop of London, 1520 to 1610*, Harleian Society (1887), p. 26.

3. Prerogative Court of Canterbury, 7 Noodes; abstract in *North Country Wills*, Surtees Society (1908), I, 238–240.

olde woman that she was a spaniards birde & he said to her that the best learned man in Englande coulde not say so much in xxiiij hours studye but that she had the devell aboute her. . . .

The last "she" of course refers to the witch of Norwell. Anne then asked him whether what the witch said was true, and Watson, playing for time to devise an impressive story,

tooke aduisem^t to answeare her & after iij or iiij^{or} dayes he comeinge to her she sware to him that if he did tell her the witches meaneinge by a spaniard*es* birde she would neuer reveale him & then he toulde her that the best spaniard that euer came in England was her father & toulde her that she had mark*es* aboute her y^t should appeare greater hereafter & that she should haue a locke of heare like gold wyer in her heade & a marke in the nape of her necke like the *lett*re M & three moles standeing triangle vpon her right shoulder & vpon the Reynes of her backe she should haue a marke of the breadeth of two pence wch in time should growe to a greater compasse & she sayeth that from that time she tooke the veiwe thereof in a glasse & there appeared a redd spott of the breadeth of a two pence vpon the Reynes of her backe & since Witsontide last it did appeare the breadeth of both her hand*es* & as it seemed to her of the forme of a Rundell haueinge on the one side a Lion & on thother side a dragon & a Crowne on the toppe & beinge asked what was the name of him that toulde her this she refuseth to tell his name because she had made an othe to the Contrarye.

What Anne imagined she saw, then, was not precisely the arms of England (three lions quartered with the lilies of France), as the witch had foretold, but it was close enough: a roundel crowned (like the lion crest of England) and sustained by the royal supporters, the lion and the dragon of the Tudors, which had not yet given place to Scotland's unicorn.

Now might Mistress Burnell well be the proudest woman in the parish; but alas! her husband, whom she had hoped to astonish, was not properly impressed:

And farther she sayeth that since Witsontide last her husbande vpbradeinge her wth the basenes of her parentage her father beinge one Kirkall a Butcher in Eastcheape in London who died xiiij yeares past & her mother long before: she answeared him it might be she was a better gentlewoman then any Burnell in Englande was a gent*leman* sayeing as it was toulde her she was kinge Phillips childe although she made no greate accompte thereof & she wished him to look vpon the Reynes of her backe who at the first p*er*ceived nothinge but veynes: but aboute a fourthnight after he looked on her backe & said he saw the Armes of Englande & fell a laugheinge & she asked him why he laughed & he said because she was branded on the backe as one of the Queens greate horses was on the Buttocke.

It sounds as though her husband had decided that the best way to deal with her fancy was to laugh her out of it; but even this device did not succeed. Asked whether any others had seen the mark, she said she had shown it to divers who had both seen it and told her that they saw it — perhaps in order to pacify her. It was long ere she would confess who these persons were, but at length she named Johan Fenton and Elizabeth Bradshawe, who, she said, "if theye weare put to theire booke othe would confesse as much." She added, Dalton records,

that the saide marke doth not at all times appeare but com*m*only at the full of the moone & because it was full moone theighte of August I caused my wife, Mrs Warner the said Johan ffenton & Elizabeth Bradshawe to veiwe her bodye who after they had seene it affirmed they sawe no apparaunce of any such marke but a greate nomber of veines.

Johan, wife of John Fenton of Holborn, tailor, though

sworn on the request of Anne, nevertheless testified that she on "veiweinge the body of the said Anne could perceive no such thinge . . . & this she said & deposed to her face & also she perswaded her to put that conceite out of her minde for she was abused much therin." Thomas Bradeshaw of Holborn, barber, and his wife Elizabeth, said that Anne had showed them the place, in modest manner, and that they likewise had perceived nothing. All the witnesses agreed that Anne had told them she was King Philip's child but that they had never understood her to say that she was Queen Mary's, "but rather to be base borne."

In her examination, Anne faithfully kept her promise not to reveal the name of the "gentleman that was said to be very well learned" who had told her "that the best Spaniard that ever came in England was her father" and of the marvelous marks that "should appear greater hereafter." Watson had been careful to bind her by an oath, for he had no desire to get into trouble for soothsaying — or for conycatching. But she had mentioned his name to Elizabeth Bradeshawe, who deposed: "She toulde her that there was one Watson a wise man in St Ellenes that could tell strange thinges whome she sent for but coulde not be founde he shoulde haue toulde her her fortune if he had come." Dalton, with messengers or sergeants to rely on, was more successful than she in tracing out Watson, but even so it appears to have taken him four days.

The wise man of St. Helen's was wise enough, as we have seen, not to say anything that could implicate himself in the least. He knows the lady, certainly, very well; he did hear her talk of something told her by an old woman that dwelt in the country; but to this speech "he

sayeth he said nothinge." The impression he gives is
that he, as a learned man, was above discussing such
trifles as these old wives' tales. He can deny with alacrity
that he had ever said she was King Philip's or Queen
Mary's child. He knew the proper style of an oracle better
than to say anything so explicit. As for the rest, he denies
it all very coolly. Tom Watson, who lived by his wits,
was not the man to accuse himself when there was no
stronger testimony against him than that of a woman
somewhat touched by the moon. Yet it was his smooth
tongue, beginning perhaps only with a compliment ("if
she knewe her selfe she would be the proudest woman in the
parishe") that gave outline and color to the vague hints of
the witch of Norwell, and built castles in Spain that lasted
in the mind of Anne Burnell for thirteen years. No doubt
she rewarded him for his fortune-telling; and indeed he
deserved, like the witch, at least a band and a bracelet,
though of iron rather than amber. To her, however, there
may have been a greater pleasure than that of gold or orna-
ments in what he had given her: the illusion of greatness.

After Watson came Dalton's wife Mary, who deposed
that she also had known Anne for eight years and that she

first came acquainted wth her by occasion she did lie at one M^{rs}
Burnels house her mother in lawe a nere neighboure to her &
a gentlewoman to whome she was much behouldeinge & there
conceaved a good likeinge of her both for her modesty & good behaviour & also for her gentlewomanlye qualityes toucheinge
workes whearein she taketh much pleasure & for that cause she
hath given her entertaynem^t before this time very often & many
times to her abilitye hath releaved her necessityes & for the
same respectes nowe hath received her into her house: She
saieth that she hearde her saye that she hath bin boorne in hande
that she was kinge Phillips Childe at wch so sone as she heard

she smiled at it & said familiarly she was a foole: & the said Mrs Burnell toulde her that she had the mark*es* of the Armes of Englande on her bodye & that she should see them & she shewed her her bodye & there she coulde *per*ceive no suche thinge & toulde her she was abused & rated her for it & willed her to take heede of such matters & toulde her it woulde torne her to trouble.

This episode occurred about three weeks past, when Anne Burnell first came to the Daltons. Since then she had never spoken of it, but behaved herself very modestly and virtuously and been very quiet till her late examination.

Finally, Dalton himself, since the Council wished his opinion of her conversation and behavior, said that he had ever thought very well of her:

But I *per*swade my selfe she hath bin much deluded wch I very much pitty & do suspecte the same *par*telye to haue ben by evell acquaintaunce she gott while her husbande was prisonner in the king*es* benche wheare it seemeth she hath bin practized to be drawen to sup*er*stic*i*on & such like vanitye: but since she came to my howse her behaviour hath bin very good & vertuous much given to prayer & abstinence & to good gentlewomanlye exercises all the day without resorte to her of anye or goeing abrode but in my wiues company . . . she seemeth much enclined to melancholye & to haue phantasticall imaginac*i*ons of the sight of such thing*es* as noone that I can heare as yet can see besides herselfe & I am not without doubte of worse effect*es* of that humor specially if she should come amonge such evell people as woulde feede her humor as amonge such it seemeth she hath bin to much alreadye: it semeth that her witt*es* be troubled & through greate misery & penury & a late flighteinge vpon the late trouble of her husbande & herselfe are greatelye decayed: she is weake & taketh no rest a night*es*: And this is all that I can as yet enforme yor hono^{rs} of her.

The "superstition" to which she was drawn was not her belief in witches and wise men but in Roman Catholicism. In 1578, for example, "Edward Burnell, an Irishe man," was arrested by the Dean and Mayor of Canterbury and sent up to the Lords of the Council, in charge of Richard Kidde, with "sundrie books and munimentes of supersticion contrarie to the presente state of Relligion established in this realme." A Burnell was already a prisoner in the Tower in 1577, and two years later the Council ordered Sir Owen Hopton to deliver Edward Burnell to the custody of the Knight Marshal.[1] Walsingham sent a Burnell to Fotheringay to carry the warrant for the execution of Mary Queen of Scots;[2] but Anne's husband was more probably the "Mr Burnell" who was imprisoned after the Babington plot in September, 1586.[3] This would explain "the late trouble of her husbande and herselfe," which Dalton speaks of in 1587, and which, with his imprisonment in the Queen's Bench, had caused her wits to be "greately decayed."

When Babington and his fellow-conspirators were captured, the citizens of London rang the church bells and made bonfires and banquets in the streets to show their rejoicing for the Queen's safety. Elizabeth wrote a letter of thanks which was read before a great assembly in the Guildhall, and Stow[4] prints at length "Master James Dalton his Oration" on this occasion, which expresses the contemporary feeling against "immoderate affecters of the Romish religion, and superstitions," who "haue become inventors of mischiefes, bruiters and spreaders abrod of false and seditious rumors, such as ioy at no good thing." The "immoderate" here is characteristic of the

1. *Acts of the Privy Council*, X (1895), 58, 245 f., 251; XI (1895), 102.
2. Historical MSS. Commission, *Calendar of the MSS. . . . at Hatfield House*, III (1889), 217.
3. *Publications of the Catholic Record Society*, II (1906), 257.
4. *The Annales or Generall Chronicle of England* (1615), pp. 727 f.

Elizabethan attitude toward religion; but Dalton himself had once been "immoderate" enough, in the last year when Catholicism was in power, to be expelled from Lincoln's Inn for suspicion of heresy. Twenty years later, when he was Treasurer of the Inn, his fellow-benchers ordered that the record of expulsion, "for that it was odiously prosequuted and odiously regestred in the tyme of Popery, must be vtterly blotted out and putt to perpetuall oblyvion." The Black Book shows it blotted out, but not quite utterly.[1] When Dalton examined Watson, he was "one of the Counsellers of the City," and in 1594 Burghley secured him the office of under-sheriff of London. In July of that year rumor deceived him into informing the aldermen that Burghley was dead. The weary Lord Treasurer wrote his son Robert that he wished it were true, and that soon it was likely to be.[2] Dalton would be better known to-day if he had ever finished his work on the government of London, to which Stow thus refers: "being informed that a learned gentleman (*Iames Dalton*) a Citizen borne, minded such a labour, and promised to performe it, I haue forborne, and left the same to his good leysure: but hee being now lately deceased" (in 1601), Stow had to write it for himself. Kingsford suggests that Dalton may have been the author of "A Discourse of the names and first causes of the institution of Cities and peopled townes," otherwise called "An Apologie of the Cittie of London," printed by Stow and evidently written by an antiquarian lawyer at the time of the 1580 proclamation against increasing the size of

---

1. *The Records of the Honourable Society of Lincoln's Inn, The Black Books,* I (1897), 323, 408.
2. Lansdowne MS. 77, nos. 31, 51; S. P. Dom. Eliz. 249/33.

London by erecting new buildings.[1] Dalton is the un-
named bencher of Lincoln's Inn to whom Sir John Harington intends an allusion in *The Metamorphosis of Ajax*
(1596),[2] as is made clear by two references to Master
Dalton the same year in *Ulysses upon Ajax*.[3]

Anne Burnell, unfortunately, did not always remain
in such kind hands as those of Dalton. Her delusion had
become deep-rooted by time and imprisonment, though
it did not originate, as one historian has conjectured, in
the strain of the threatened Spanish invasion after the
defeat of the Armada.[4] She continued to proclaim herself
a daughter of Philip of Spain, and her servant Alice Digges
vouched for the presence of the royal arms on her back.
Late in 1592, after Watson was dead, her case came before
the Privy Council, who wrote the following letter to the
Lord Mayor:[5]

We have receaved from yo^w the Examinacion of An*n*e Burnell
wth the certificat*es* of the Phisitians and Chirurgeon, and finde
hereby that her Allegac*i*on of the Armes of Englande and
Spayne to be seene on her backe, is false and proceedinge of some
lewde and imposterouse p^rtence, aswell in her as in Allice Digges
her woman avowchinge that shee hath seene the same in the
backe of her Mistres; in respect whereof, and that shee Contin-
neweth in her vaine opinion sayinge she is the daughter of Kinge
Phillip, we thinke it mete they both receave som publike pun-
ishm^t. and therefore doe requyre yo^w vppon the next Markett

---

1. *A Survey of London*, ed. Kingsford (1908), II, 186, 386 f.
2. Sig. G 6^v.
3. Signatures D 1^v, D 5^v. He is mentioned also in F. A. Inderwick, *A Calendar of the Inner Temple Records*, I (1896), 473; Hotson, *Shakespeare versus Shallow*, p. 180; and E 179/251/16, the subsidy roll for 1582, where he and "Mrs Burnell widowe" are each assessed on twenty pounds in lands in the parish of Aldermanbury.
4. R. R. Sharpe, *London and the Kingdom* (1894), I, 552.
5. Guildhall Records, Journal 23, f. 153.

day to cawse the said Ann Burnell and Allice Digges (there backes only beeinge layde bare) to be well whipped at the tayle of a Carte through the Citty wth a note in writinge vppon the hinder parte of there heades shewinge the cawse of there saide punishm^{te}, and this shalbe yor warraunt in that behalf. Soe fare yo^{w} well. from hampton Courte the xth of December. 1592.

At the request of the Lord Mayor and his brethren, Burghley consented on December 12 that the punishment for "the younge wenche Anne Digges," as he names her, might be forborne and replaced by some other correction.

Contemporary journalism and history both took care to record Anne Burnell's strange hallucination. The brother-in-law of Thomas Lodge, Edward White, satisfied people's desire to hear of it by publishing a ballad, entered at Stationers' Hall on December 18.[1] The title seemed to the company's clerk important enough to record in full:

a ballad shewinge how a fond woman falsely accused her self to be the kinge of Spaines daughter and beinge founde a lyer was for the same whipped through London the xiiijth of December 1592 beinge known to be a butchers daughter of London.

The whipping occurred on December 13, according to Stow's chronicle:

The 13. of December a certayne Gentlewoman by the Counsells commaundement was whipped through the Citty of London for affirming herselfe to bee the daughter of *Phillip* K of Spayne, as shee had beene perswaded by some accompted south-sayers, after prooued liers, for shee was knowne to bee a butchers daughter in East Cheape.[2]

---

1. Edward Arber, *A Transcript of the Registers of the Company of Stationers of London*, II (1875), 624.

2. *The Annales* (1615), p. 764. Compare Hyder E. Rollins, *An Analytical Index to the Ballad-Entries in the Registers of the Company of Stationers of London* (*Studies in Philology*, XXI [1924], 209–210).

It must be remembered that what Dalton sent to Burghley was a set of examinations taken down by his clerk, so that we do not have a deposition by Watson with a signature which would positively identify him. A "Thomas Watson, yom*an*" appears as a resident of St. Helen's, Bishopsgate, in a list sent to Burghley of "Names of Strangers that goe not to churche, 24 Junij," 1581.[1] This may conceivably be the poet, in view of the Catholic leanings indicated by his travels on the Continent and his sojourn at Douai a few years earlier.

I find a later Thomas Watson, gentleman, who had a daughter Elizabeth christened at St. Helen's on May 22, 1597.[2] There is no record of him in the parish before or afterward. He might naturally be supposed to have been the wise man in question, were it not that the examinant happens to mention that he had been at Oxford before 1579. A Thomas Watson of Worcestershire, aged nineteen, matriculated from St. Mary's Hall on May 26, 1580,[3] and entered the Middle Temple on November 26, 1581, as son and heir of Nicholas Watson of Worcestershire, gentleman.[4] The Oxford registers preserve no record of any other Thomas Watson at all in Elizabeth's reign. We know, however, that the poet was an Oxford man; for in his Latin verses to Greene's *Ciceronis Amor* in 1589 he describes himself as "*Thomas Watson*, Oxon."[5] The evidence, then, seems to point to our Watson as the

1. Lansdowne MS. 33, no. 59, printed by R. E. G. Kirk and E. F. Kirk, *Returns of Aliens, The Publications of the Huguenot Society of London*, X, ii (1902), 220.

2. *Harleian Society Registers*, XXXI (1904), 7.

3. Andrew Clark, *Register of the University of Oxford*, II, ii (1887), 93.

4. C. T. Martin, *Minutes of Parliament of the Middle Temple*, I (1904), 246.

5. A. B. Grosart, *The Life and Complete Works in Prose and Verse of Robert Greene*, VII (1881–83), 103.

"gentleman that was said to be very well learned." The description certainly fits the promising young Latinist; whereas if any other Thomas Watson had a reputation as a scholar, no record of it has come down to us. Proof is out of the question, and we can only trust to probabilities. As our information stands at present, the poet is the one Oxford man whom the glove seems to fit, and it is reasonable to accept the identification if we do so tentatively and subject to increase of knowledge.

Apparently, therefore, in 1587, the year of Marlowe's coming up from Cambridge to London and his services in affairs of state, Watson was living in St. Helen's, Bishopsgate. Bishopsgate is precisely the quarter of London in which we should expect to find him, in view of his tutorship to the son of William Cornwallis of Bishopsgate, and his later residence in Norton Folgate, near at hand. It appears also that in 1579, the year of *The Shepherds' Calendar*, the Areopagus letter, and Spenser's residence in Westminster, Watson used to lodge there with his Oxford friend Mr. Beale, a preacher, at the house of one Waller. The register of St. Margaret's, Westminster, shows a Rafe Waller buried on September 28, 1579, and an Edward Waller, who had several children christened between 1564 and 1573, buried on February 26, 1583/4. The Oxford registers establish Watson's friend Mr. Beale as a William Beale, one of two Williams who had taken degrees at Oxford, since no other Christian name appears until 1583. If he was a contemporary of Watson, he was the William Beale who secured his B.A. on July 29, 1574, and determined in 1574/5. An earlier William took his B.A. in 1562, his M.A. in 1565/6, and supplicated for the B.D. in 1572, in which year one of his name was rector of West

Horsley, Surrey.[1] A William Beale held the prebend of Shalford in Wells Cathedral in 1576, but not in 1579.[2] At the time of Watson's examination his Oxford friend was no longer living, for "William Bele, clerk," was buried at St. Margaret's, Westminster, on September 20, 1582.[3]

Marlowe is said to have "translated Coluthus's *Rape of Helen* into English rhyme, in the year 1587," according to "the manuscript papers of a diligent collector of these fugacious anecdotes," Thomas Coxeter (d. 1747).[4] Warton adds, "I have never seen it," nor has any later writer. W. C. Hazlitt declares that "Coxeter was a remorseless forger of titles and facts."[5] On the other hand, it is possible that Marlowe's poem has disappeared since Coxeter's time. Watson's Latin translation of the same Greek original survives only in a single copy which happens to be preserved in the University Library at Cambridge. Watson published the book in 1586 with the following title-page: "COLVTHI THE- | BANI LYCOPOLI- | TANI POETÆ, | *Helenæ Raptus* | Latinus, Paraphraste | Thoma Watsono Londinensi. | [device][6] | LONDINI | Apud Iohannem Wolfium. | 1586." He dedicated the poem "Ad Illustrissimum D. Dominum Henricum Perseum, Comitem Northumbriæ" — not "Duke of Northumberland," as Watson's biographers persist in calling him. To the account of

1. Joseph Foster, *Alumni Oxonienses*, I (1891), 95.

2. J. Le Neve, *Fasti Ecclesiae Anglicanae* (1854), I, 200.

3. A. M. Burke, *Memorials of St. Margaret's Church, Westminster* (1914), p. 441.

4. Thomas Warton, *History of English Poetry* (1871), IV, 310. See Tucker Brooke, "The Marlowe Canon," *P.M.L.A.*, XXXVII (1922), 414; and L. C. Martin, *Marlowe's Poems* (1931), p. 22.

5. Warton, *History of English Poetry* (1871), IV, 210 n.

6. Number 242 in R. B. McKerrow, *Printers' and Publishers' Devices in England and Scotland, 1485–1640* (1913).

Northumberland recently given by Dr. Harrison I may
add that I have found among Sir Julius Caesar's papers a
brief essay by the Earl, not hitherto known, entitled "My
Lord of Northumberlands conceipt concerning Friends
and Friendshipp." [1]

Watson also presented to Northumberland an unpub-
lished translation, which has never been mentioned by the
poet's biographers, entitled "*A learned Dialogue of Bernard
Palessy, Concerning waters and fountaines, both naturall and
artificiall:* Translated Owt of French into English, by
Thomas Watson." [2] Of this manuscript, bought in 1928 by
Messrs. Quaritch and Company, I have given a description
elsewhere in connection with a study of two Watson
manuscripts in the British Museum, Harleian MS. 3277
and Sloane MS. 3731.

1. British Museum Additional MS. 12,504, folios 54^r–58^r.
2. *Sixth Report of the Royal Commission on Historical Manuscripts* (1877),
p. 310; Sotheby and Co., *Catalogue of Exceedingly Rare and Valuable Americana,
with Some Important English Books & Manuscripts, Largely from the Library of
Henry Percy, 9th Earl of Northumberland (1564–1632), at Petworth House* (1928,
April 23–24, lot 112), p. 48.

CHAPTER IX

A Dedication by Marlowe

THE records of Chancery and of Middlesex Sessions have furnished unusually full solutions to two of the questions proposed at the beginning of this inquiry: where Marlowe lived in London, and what was the cause of his unexplained appearance at Newgate. Perhaps most interesting of all is their answer to the remaining question: with which of the poets of his time did Marlowe find companionship? In 1591 he was writing in the same chamber with Kyd, but there is no very clear evidence concerning the degree of his friendship with other writers, though Nashe, Peele, and Greene must have been among his associates. Watson, whose patron and old friend was Thomas Walsingham, would naturally come into close relationship with Marlowe. Their friendship, which already could be seen to be probable, has been put beyond question by the discovery that the two poets took the sword in turn against a common enemy.

The establishing of Marlowe's friendship with Watson enables us to make a small yet interesting addition to the canon of his works. Mr. Brooke has recently remarked [1] that Marlowe "did not resort in any published work to the usual recourse of the indigent poet, dedication to the great or wealthy." As a matter of fact, he was killed before any of his works came to the press except *Tambur-*

[1]. *The Life of Marlowe*, p. 38.

laine, edited and published by Richard Jones in 1590. Since it was not the custom in Elizabeth's reign for a professional dramatist to publish what he wrote for the stage, Marlowe had no occasion to dedicate any of his plays. Poems were a different matter. As Shakespeare of all his works wrote dedications only for *Venus and Adonis* and *The Rape of Lucrece,* so Marlowe in all likelihood would have published *Hero and Leander,* if he had lived to finish it, with the usual dedication. Probably his patron would have been Thomas Walsingham, to whom Edward Blount in 1598 dedicated the fragment in an attempt to carry out Marlowe's wishes.

That Marlowe was not too proud and aloof to praise the great or wealthy can be clearly shown. There has long been known a dedication of the *Amintæ Gaudia* of Watson, entered in the Stationers' Register on November 10, 1592, which bears the signature "C. M." Watson had just died, and his friend "C. M.," who can only be Christopher Marlowe, therefore commended this "Posthumus Amyntas" to the protection of the Countess of Pembroke. Writers on Watson have generally suggested, more or less doubtfully, the possibility that the initials were those of Marlowe.[1] Writers on Marlowe have paid no attention whatever to the suggestion, with two exceptions. Mr. Brooke mentions it, only to dismiss it with the remark, "There is small reason to suppose that Marlowe ever

1. Thomas Park, *The Gentleman's Magazine,* LXVIII (1798), ii, 669; J. P. Collier, *A Bibliographical and Critical Account of the Rarest Books in the English Language* (1865), II, 490; W. C. Hazlitt, *Hand-Book to the Popular, Poetical, and Dramatic Literature of Great Britain* (1867), p. 645; Arber, *Thomas Watson, Poems* (1870), p. 14; Thomas Corser, *Collectanea Anglo-Poetica,* Chetham Society, CXI (1883), 377; W. W. Greg, "English Versions of Watson's Latin Poems," *The Modern Language Quarterly,* VI (1903), 125, 128; M. A. Scott, *Elizabethan Translations from the Italian* (1916), p. 139.

belonged to the Countess of Pembroke's circle." [1]   Miss Ellis-Fermor lists the book, under the strange title of "*Amintæ Gandiæ*," among works that "have been wrongly attributed to him and are now rejected by the majority of his biographers." [2]   It is odd that none of the biographers has noticed Watson's connection with Thomas Walsingham.   No other "C. M." has ever been put forward, and there is no reason whatever for impugning the identification with Marlowe.   What formerly was hypothesis is now placed beyond reasonable doubt by the new testimony to Marlowe's close association with Watson.

Since it was "the right honourable the Earl of Pembroke his servants" who acted *Edward II*, probably in this same year of 1592, it is not easy to see why the Countess of Pembroke's circle should be regarded as a magic one which Marlowe could not have entered.   Sidney's sister was the most generous of patronesses, and Marlowe had certainly as good a right as any man to desire her patronage.   Too close a connection is often supposed between a poet and the person to whom he dedicated books.   The patron of a company of actors, such as Pembroke was, had at least given his consent to the players' becoming his men.   An author, feeding like the chameleon on airy hope, might, on the other hand, put his patron's name in the front of his book without any certainty that the dedication would be accepted.   It is not necessary to assume, then, that Marlowe revolved in Mary Sidney's special circle. But it is pleasant to know that he praised her and that he believed his praise would not be unwelcome.

Since the dedication has never appeared in any edition

1. "The Marlowe Canon," *P. M. L. A.*, XXXVII (1922), 414.
2. *Christopher Marlowe* (1927), p. 9.

of Marlowe's works, and has not been translated, I print in full Marlowe's own words, now recovered for him, and a suggested English rendering:

Illustrissimæ Heroinæ omnibus et animi et corporis dotibus ornatissimæ, Mariæ Penbrokiæ Comitissæ.

Laurigera stirpe prognata Delia, Sydnæi vatis Apollinei genuina [1] soror; Alma literarum parens, ad cuius immaculatos amplexus, confugit virtus, barbariei & ignorantiae impetu violata, vt olim a Threicio Tyranno Philomela; Poetarum nostri temporis, ingeniorumque omnium fœlicissime pullulantium,[2] Musa; Dia proles, quæ iam rudi calamo, spiritus infundis elati furoris, quibus ipse misellus, plus mihi videor præstare posse, quam cruda nostra indoles proferre solet: Dignare Posthumo huic Amyntæ, vt tuo adoptiuo filio patrocinari: Eoque magis quòd moribundus pater, illius tutelam humillimè tibi legauerat. Et licet illustre nomen tuum non solùm apud nos, sed exteras etiam nationes, latius propagatum est, quàm aut vnquàm possit æruginosa Temporis vetustate aboleri, aut mortalium encomijs augeri, (quomodò enim quicquam possit esse infinito plus?) multorum tamèn camænis, quasi siderum diademate redimita *Ariadne*, noli hunc purum Phœbi sacerdotem, stellam alteram coronæ tuæ largientem, aspernari: sed animi candore, quem sator hominum, atque deorum, Iupiter, prænobili familiæ tuæ quasi hæreditarium[3] alligauit, accipe, & tuere. Sic nos, quorum opes tenuissimæ,[3] littorea sunt Myrtus Veneris, Nymphæque Peneiæ semper virens coma, prima quaque poematis pagina, Te Musarum dominam, in auxilium invocabimus: tua denique virtus, quæ virtutem ipsam, ipsam quoque æternitatem superabit.

Honoris tui studiosissimus, C. M.

1. Emended from *genuuia*.
2. Emended from *pullutantium*.
3. Printed incorrectly by Edward Arber, *Thomas Watson, Poems* (1870), p. 14.

To the Most Illustrious Noble Lady, adorned with all gifts both of mind and body, Mary Countess of Pembroke.

Delia born of a laurel-crowned race, true sister of Sidney the bard of Apollo; fostering parent of letters, to whose immaculate embrace virtue, outraged by the assault of barbarism and ignorance, flieth for refuge, as once Philomela from the Thracian tyrant; Muse of the Poets of our time, and of all most happily burgeoning wits; descendant of the gods, who impartest now to my rude pen breathings of a lofty rage, whereby my poor self hath, methinks, power to surpass what my unripe talent is wont to bring forth: Deign to be patron to this posthumous Amyntas, as to thine adoptive son: the rather that his dying father had most humbly bequeathed to thee his keeping. And though thy glorious name is spread abroad not only among us but even among foreign nations, too far ever to be destroyed by the rusty antiquity of Time, or added to by the praise of mortals (for how can anything be greater than what is infinite?), yet, crowned as thou art by the songs of many as by a starry diadem Ariadne, scorn not this pure priest of Phoebus bestowing another star upon thy crown: but with that sincerity of mind which Jove the father of men and of gods hath linked as hereditary to thy noble family, receive and watch over him. So shall I, whose slender wealth is but the seashore myrtle of Venus, and Daphne's evergreen laurel, on the foremost page of every poem invoke thee as Mistress of the Muses to my aid: to sum up all, thy virtue, which shall overcome virtue herself, shall likewise overcome even eternity.

> Most desirous to do thee honor,
> C. M.

Mary Sidney, "the subject of all verse," had taken her place as "Muse of the poets of our time and of all most happily burgeoning wits" ever since Thomas Howell dedicated to her his *Devises* in 1581. But in the years from 1591 to 1593 she received more dedications than in all the rest of her life, and in 1592 she was at the very height of her glory. These were the years during which she showed the most active interest in literature. *The Countess of Pembroke's Arcadia*, Sidney's romance, had been published without her consent in 1590; she issued her corrected edition in 1593. In 1590 she finished Sidney's translation from du Plessis de Mornay and translated Garnier's tragedy of *Antonie* (both entered in the Stationers' Register May 3, 1592).

Spenser dedicated to the Countess of Pembroke *The Ruins of Time* (S. R. December 29, 1590). Nashe followed with his preface to the first edition of Sidney's *Astrophel and Stella* (1591). Abraham Fraunce addressed to her in the same year *The Countess of Pembroke's Emanuel* and *The Countess of Pembroke's Ivychurch*. Nicholas Breton praised her in his dedication of *The Pilgrimage to Paradise* (S. R. January 23, 1590/91), published in 1592 together with *The Countess of Pembroke's Love*. In 1592 she received also the dedications of Daniel's *Delia* (S. R. February 4), Fraunce's *Amintas' Dale* (October 2), and Watson's *Amintæ Gaudia* (November 10). Next year Barnabe Barnes wrote her a sonnet as one of the patrons of *Parthenophil and Parthenope*, and Thomas Morley dedicated to her his *Canzonets*, while in 1594 Daniel sent her his *Cleopatra* to bear her *Antonie* company. In the same year Kyd published his *Cornelia*, a tragedy which he had translated, following the example of Lady Pembroke, from Robert Garnier.

Marlowe, therefore, had every reason to hope that the Countess of Pembroke would look on his dedication with favor. But there was also a special reason why Watson should, as Marlowe says he did, bequeath to her his pastoral poems on the joys of Amintas. The first book dedicated to her by Sidney's friend and schoolfellow, Abraham Fraunce, *The Lamentations of Amyntas* (1587), was mainly an English rendering of Watson's Latin: not, as Mary Sidney's biographer supposes,[1] his *Amintæ Gaudia*, which was not yet written, but his *Amyntas*, published in 1585. In his preface to *Meliboeus* (1590) Watson called public attention to the fact that Fraunce had not acknowledged the use of Watson's work.   Fraunce accordingly mentioned Watson's name when in 1591 he republished his poems on Amyntas as part of *The Countess of Pembroke's Ivychurch*. Watson naturally wished to share in the favor his translator was securing from the Countess, who seems to have been particularly interested in poems on Amyntas. But before he had written his dedication for *Amintæ Gaudia*, death took him off, and it was left for Marlowe to carry out his friend's desire.

Just before Marlowe wrote his dedication of Watson's "posthumous Amyntas," Fraunce published yet another volume on Amyntas: *The Third Part of the Countesse of Pembrokes Yuychurch: Entituled, Amintas Dale*. The book is a collection of "the most conceited tales of the Pagan Gods," and one of the stories told in verse is that of Venus and Adonis. Venus recites to Adonis "How *Leander* dyde, as he swamme to the bewtiful Hero." The teller of the tale, "faire Cassiopeia," makes an interesting comment on the popularity of the story which Marlowe retold: "*Leander* and *Heroes* loue is in euery mans mouth . . . *Ouid* in his epistles passionately setteth it downe, and *Boscan* hath made a whole volume of it in Spanish, entituled *Historia de Leandro y Hero*," of which she quotes the opening lines.[2]

1. Frances Berkeley Young, *Mary Sidney, Countess of Pembroke* (1912), p. 162.

2. Signatures M 2, M 4.

Marlowe probably saw *Amintas' Dale* shortly before he wrote the dedication of *Amintæ Gaudia*, for he appears to have taken over and elaborated the opening phrase of Fraunce's dedication, "Illustrissimæ, atque ornatissimæ Heroinæ." The borrower is less likely to have been Fraunce, both because his book was entered in the Stationers' Register over a month earlier than Watson's, and because Marlowe certainly made use of some phrases by "well-languaged Daniel." In 1591/2 Daniel dedicated *Delia* to the Countess of Pembroke, "whome the fortune of our time hath made the happie and iudiciall Patronesse of the Muses, (a glory hereditary to your house) to preserue them from those hidious Beestes, Obliuion and Barbarisme." Daniel's words may have stuck in Marlowe's mind quite unconsciously when he echoed them in Latin. They show that before embarking on his dedication he had taken care to read what other poets had said to the Countess. Marlowe's dedication was read, in its turn, by later poets, for Charles Fitzgeoffrey published in 1601 a poem "Ad Illustrissimam Heroinam *Mariam Pembrochiæ* Comitissam"[1] beginning, "*Sydnæi* genuina soror," the very words of Marlowe in *Amintæ Gaudia*. The dedication is the first writing by Marlowe that has been traced in America, for among the books of John Harvard, which formed the nucleus of Harvard College Library, the catalogue lists "Watsonj animæ Gaudia."[2]

In 1594 *Amintæ Gaudia* was partly translated by a certain "I. T. gent.," who writes that "perusing (at idle howers) the author of *Amintas* ioyes," he found the Latin not unmeet "to be clothed with an English suit," under the

---

1. *Affaniæ*, sig. G 7.
2. *Publications of the Colonial Society of Massachusetts*, XXI (1919), 227; T. G. Wright, *Literary Culture in Early New England* (1920), p. 272.

title of "*An Ould Facioned Love. Or a love of the Ould facion.*" [1] Only two copies of the book are known, one in the Capell collection at Trinity College, Cambridge, the other at Sion College in London. I shall discuss elsewhere the interesting question whether "I. T. gent." was the John Trussell who in 1595 published another imitative poem, *The First Rape of the Fair Helen*, following in the footsteps of Shakespeare, "Watsons heyre."

The discovery in Chancery and Middlesex Sessions Rolls of the full story of Marlowe's adventure with the law in 1589 at last clears the poet's reputation from the shadow of supposed felony. Marlowe was not indicted for felony, as scholars believed when they knew only that he was bound over to answer charges at the Gaol Delivery of Newgate. He was arrested on suspicion of murder, because he had begun the fight with William Bradley which his fellow-poet Watson ended by plunging six inches of steel into Bradley's breast. But the coroner's jury declared that Watson struck the mortal blow for the saving of his own life, "et non per feloniam." Marlowe was freed on the bail of Richard Kitchen and Humphrey Rowland, kept his pledge to reappear at the Old Bailey, and was discharged according to law. Watson received the Queen's pardon *se defendendo*, as Ingram Frizer did for the killing of Marlowe.

Bradley, son of the innkeeper at the Bishop in High Holborn, was a young swashbuckler who had already quarreled with Watson. If Marlowe had not been quick to defend himself, he might have ended his career at the age of twenty-five instead of twenty-nine, and left behind no

1. Cf. William Beloe, *Anecdotes of Literature and Scarce Books*, II (1807), 70–71; Greg in *The Modern Language Quarterly*, VI (1903), 128–129.

Edward II or *The Jew of Malta*, perhaps not even his masterpieces *Hero and Leander* and *Dr. Faustus*.

Marlowe and Watson crossed swords with Bradley in Hog Lane, which ran through Finsbury Fields north of the present Finsbury Square, not far from Finsbury Pavement, where Keats was born. The list of prisoners in Newgate has given an answer to the problem of Marlowe's residence in London. In 1589 he lived in the liberty of Norton Folgate, between Bishopsgate and Shoreditch, conveniently near to the Theater and the Curtain. Three years later Marlowe attacked or threatened to attack the constables of Holywell Street, the players' quarter of Shoreditch, where Shakespeare and Greene were probably living at the time.

The new documents have shown that one of Marlowe's closest friends, the companion for whom he fought in Finsbury Fields, was the poet Thomas Watson. The only writing which Marlowe lived to publish was the dedication he composed in 1592 for Watson's *Amintæ Gaudia*. Like Marlowe, Watson made his living by writing plays, the identification of which sets criticism a difficult but not impossible problem. Further knowledge of his life may lead to further knowledge about Marlowe, for Watson had attended the English Catholic seminary in France to which Marlowe proposed to go, according to report, in 1587. Watson had family connections with two of Sir Francis Walsingham's adroitest spies, and his friendship with Thomas Walsingham provided an opening which probably led to that gentleman's patronage of Marlowe and perhaps even to Marlowe's original employment on secret service.

INDEX

INDEX